Imaginary Plots and Political Realities in the Plays of William Congreve

Figure 1 Portrait of Congreve, Richard van Bleeck (1715). Leuven, Stedjick Museum

Imaginary Plots and Political Realities in the Plays of William Congreve

Maximillian E. Novak

ANTHEM PRESS

Anthem Press
An imprint of Wimbledon Publishing Company
www.anthempress.com

This edition first published in UK and USA 2022
by ANTHEM PRESS
75–76 Blackfriars Road, London SE1 8HA, UK
or PO Box 9779, London SW19 7ZG, UK
and
244 Madison Ave #116, New York, NY 10016, USA

First published in the UK and USA by Anthem Press in 2020

Copyright © Maximillian E. Novak 2022

The author asserts the moral right to be identified as the author of this work.

All rights reserved. Without limiting the rights under copyright reserved above,
no part of this publication may be reproduced, stored or introduced into
a retrieval system, or transmitted, in any form or by any means
(electronic, mechanical, photocopying, recording or otherwise),
without the prior written permission of both the copyright
owner and the above publisher of this book.

British Library Cataloguing-in-Publication Data
A catalogue record for this book is available from the British Library.

Library of Congress Control Number: 2020936141

ISBN-13: 978-1-83998-434-1 (Pbk)
ISBN-10: 1-83998-434-1 (Pbk)

This title is also available as an e-book.

CONTENTS

List of Illustrations   vii

Acknowledgments   ix

Preface   xi

1. The Politics of Love, Marriage, and Scandal in Congreve's World   1
2. *Incognita* and Some Problems in Morality and Epistemology   17
3. The "Fashionable Cutt of the Town" and William Congreve's *The Old Batchelor*   33
4. Political and Moral Double Dealing in Congreve's *The Double Dealer*   51
5. Foresight in the Stars and Scandal in London: Reading the Hieroglyphics in Congreve's *Love for Love*   67
6. The Failure of Perception and Politics in Congreve's *The Mourning Bride*   87
7. Politics and Congreve's *The Way of the World*   101

Afterword   121

Works Cited   123

Index   129

ILLUSTRATIONS

1 Portrait of Congreve, Richard van Bleeck (1715). Leuven, Stedjick Museum — ii
2 Details. Richard van Bleeck's *Portrait of Congreve*. Leuven, Stedjick Museum. (a) Vanbrugh's *The Provoked Wife*. (b) Volume of the Philosopher George Berkeley — 16
3 Valentine Pretending Madness in Congreve's *Love for Love*. Detail of a painting by Robert Smirke (1753–1845). Maugham Collection, Holbourne Museum, Bath — 66
4 Elizabeth Barry Acting in the Role of Zara in Congreve's *The Mourning Bride*. National Trust, Smallhythe Place, Tenterden — 86

ACKNOWLEDGMENTS

Much of the research on this book was done in rare book libraries in the United States and Great Britain. I wish to thank the staffs of the following: the William Andrews Clark Memorial Library, the Young Research Library, and Special Collections, all of UCLA; the British Library, the Bodleian Library, Oxford; and the Beinecke Library of Yale University. I held a William Andrews Clark Memorial Library Professorship while completing some of the writing and research, and an annual grant from the UCLA's Committee on Research helped with other parts. Through these grants, I received help from a variety of assistants: Joseph Serrano, Jacob Klein, Charlotte Alleyne Kelly, Stephanie Centeno, Jorge de la Cruz, and Rhiannon Wilson. I am grateful for their help.

 This book represents the accumulated thinking about Congreve over years of teaching and research. My first book on Congreve, *William Congreve* (1970), had the benefit of requiring relatively clear readings of Congreve's texts. After I had published that work, I resolved to provide a more complex exposition of this brilliant playwright. As I worked on other dramatic writers of the Restoration and eighteenth century, including John Dryden, the comic playwrights of the 1670s, and Thomas Southerne, I continued to consider various aspects of Congreve's plays against the political and social background, which to my eyes they so clearly reflected. Occasionally I published some of these thoughts in the form of essays. Several of the chapters in this book appeared in very different form in a variety of publications. Sections of Chapter 1 appeared in a seminar paper published by the William Andrews Clark Library. Most of Chapter 3 appeared under the same title in a Festschrift for Philip Harth, edited by Howard Weinbrot. Again, a large part of Chapter 5 appeared in a volume titled *From Renaissance to Renaissance*, edited by Laurie Fink and Robert Markley and published by the Bellflower Press. I want to thank the publishers of these essays for their permission to republish this material.

PREFACE

In 1988, when the three hundredth anniversary of "The Glorious Revolution" of 1688 was to be celebrated in Great Britain, there was a distinct lack of enthusiasm for the event. Admittedly, a few modest exhibitions were started during this period of the year, but certainly no grand celebration. Edmund Burke had presented this revolution as a mere adjustment in the English political scene—an event entirely different from the French Revolution, even before its frightening executions. There was no parading of a supposedly charming queen such as Marie Antoinette on to the scaffold. No, James II had attempted to leave, had been brought back to London, had hung about for a short time, and then simply left without anyone bothering too much about it. He did attempt several comebacks—in Ireland (he lost the Battle of the Boyne), through a possible invasion—but nothing, it seemed, very effectual. The result was a degree of ambiguity, well encapsulated in the dialogue between Uncle Toby and Corporal Trim in Laurence Sterne's *Life and Opinions of Tristram Shandy*, published in separate volumes between 1759 and 1767. In presenting a vivid description of the battle of Landen, Uncle Toby waxes enthusiastic over the courage of King William III. Corporal Trim is caught up by Uncle Toby's fervid pronouncement, "Brave,! brave by heaven! [...] he deserves a crown," by shouting, "As richly, as a thief deserves a halter." Uncle Toby decides that there is no question about Corporal Trim's loyalty and refuses to pursue any objection to this questionable analogy. But as loyal as Corporal Trim might be, we know that he was wounded in his knee at the battle of Landen, left on the battlefield, and suffered excruciating pain in his recovery. For all his loyalty and his love for Uncle Toby, then, there is clearly an unconscious process of association that suggests a degree of ambivalence and resentment toward William III.

And if the history of Congreve's time failed to arouse enthusiasm, its literary history fared even worse. Writing in the middle of the nineteenth century of Congreve and his time, Hippolyte Taine concluded that all their literature was "abortive," and that they left nothing behind but the memory of corruption. In addition, during the decades preceding the celebration of the Revolution of 1688, there had been something resembling a neo-Jacobite movement. What if Dutch William had not invaded? Might not England have been better off? Might not a different tradition of native Englishness have flourished? A somewhat utopian air of alternative history might be found in some quarters.

In 2009, 20 years after this dismal show, Steve Pincus published his book, *1688: The First Modern Revolution*. Pincus refused to accept the notion that this rebellion reflected a gradual growth of Whig ideas from the time of the Interregnum. And so far from being an anachronism, James was in the forefront of European Catholic thought. The Glorious Revolution was not a peaceful transition but an event involving considerable violence. And it involved a revolution in economics and society, "a bourgeois revolution in a social and political sense," as Pincus described it, with cultural currents that were irresistible to writers such as Congreve. The 1690s were also a time of complicated philosophical and political ideas. Certainty, complete conviction was nearly impossible to achieve. Jonathan Swift was to compose his *Tale of a Tub* during the later years of this decade, forcing his readers' minds to make attempts at reconciling concepts that were irreconcilable. Congreve did not have as complex a mind as Swift, but he was able to create a series of plays that reflected some of the same difficulties perplexing his fellow Irishman.

Chapter 1

THE POLITICS OF LOVE, MARRIAGE, AND SCANDAL IN CONGREVE'S WORLD

John Dryden, who specialized in poetry involving elaborate and occasionally exaggerated encomiums, praised William Congreve as a playwright who might equal Shakespeare. Commenting upon Congreve's second play, *The Double Dealer*, Dryden argued that Congreve's writings appeared to have the "strength" of the great Elizabethan and Jacobean playwrights combined with the "skill" of the writers of the Restoration.

> Thy first attempt an early promise made;
> That early promise this had more than paid.
>
> So bold, yet so judiciously you dare,
> That your least praise is to be regular.
> Time, place, and action may with pains be wrought,
> But genius must be born, and never can be taught.
> This is your portion, this your native store;
> Heav'n, that but once was prodigal before,
> To Shakespeare gave as much; she could not give him more.[1]

Congreve certainly had a major reputation during his lifetime. But no modern literary historian has suggested naming any part of the period in which he lived "the Age of Congreve," in the way such a designation has frequently been assigned to his contemporaries: Jonathan Swift, Daniel Defoe, Alexander Pope, or even Joseph Addison. Yet his contribution of four excellent comedies and a tragedy to the literature of the English Stage was far from insignificant. Three of his plays have been revived in productions of the National Theatre and, of course, university classes in the history of the English drama are almost certain to contain one of his comedies. If he never achieved the heights of greatness imagined by Dryden, he is still to be regarded as a major British playwright.

His importance has frequently been ascribed to his witty dialogue and the charming nature of his lovers—especially Angelica and Valentine in *Love for Love* and Millamant and Mirabell in *The Way of the World*. But much of such admiration has its origin in Charles Lamb's vision of Restoration comedy as depicting an artificial milieu having little connection with a real world of sexual desire and betrayal. Whereas Lamb viewed the stage of his own time as being deeply involved in questions of morality, he argued that Congreve's plays revealed a "privation of moral light."[2] Lamb's criticism was constructed to protect Restoration comedy from a century of attacks depicting it as entirely immoral. At a time when Coleridge and others had protested against the theaters of the time as too large for permitting any appreciation of the subtleties of great drama, Lamb's comments at least had the effect of restoring the comedies of the last 40 years of the seventeenth century as worthy of study as literature.

Since that time, Congreve and his fellow playwrights have had to weather the attack of L. C. Knights and the circle of critics about F. R. Leavis, for their lack of social awareness and the Christian readings of Aubrey Williams, which cleared Congreve of immorality but left the moral messages of his comedies little different from the morality of the saints' lives that fill the volumes of Jacobus de Voragine's *Golden Legend*. The discussion of Congreve's plays that appears in this volume will attempt to show him as very much a playwright of the 1690s, a period that inherited a complex view of social relations from 30 years of comedies that attempted to probe the complexities of sex, marriage, and love in a world in which writers such as Michel de Montaigne, René Descartes, and John Locke had opened the study of epistemology, and during that same period, the followers of Pierre Gassendi, including Thomas Hobbes, the Libertines, and the writers on natural law had provided a philosophic basis for a variety of views about human motivation. I want to begin by examining the moral milieu of Congreve's time and the preceding decades before proceeding to a view of his individual plays.

1

The last decade of the seventeenth century was a period of satire, lampoon, and libel, with the result that everyone felt just a bit irritated—the way a close circle of friends accustomed to a free exchange of sarcasm becomes after the jokes are no longer new. Even the great proviso scene of Congreve's *The Way of the World*, while it functions primarily as a poignant type of play, also operates as a general satire on love and marriage in late seventeenth-century England—and *The Way of the World* is very much about that new environment. Lady Wishfort conducts her "Cabal-Nights" at which, in Mr. Fainall's words, "they come together like the Coroner's Inquest, to sit upon the murder'd Reputations of the Week."[3] To flatter Lady Wishfort, Mirabell "got a Friend to put her into a Lampoon, and complement her with the Imputation of an Affair with a young Fellow" (Volume 2:106 [I.i, 67–68]), while Mr. Fainall's ultimate threat against his wife and mother-in-law, Lady Wishfort, is public exposure such as the divorce proceedings involving the flagrantly adulterous Duchess of Norfolk that dragged on for years in the House of Lords.[4] Mrs. Marwood conjures up a picture of such an event for Lady Wishfort:

To be ushered in with an *O Yez* of Scandal; and have your Case open'd by an old fumbling Leacher in a Quoif like a Man Midwife, to bring your Daughter's Infamy to light; to be a Theme for legal Punsters, and Quiblers by the Statute; and become a Jest, against a Rule of Court [...] Nay this is nothing; if it would end here 'twere well. But it must after this be consign'd by the Short-hand Writers to the publick Press; and from thence be transferr'd to the Hands, nay into the Throats and Lungs of Hawkers, with Voices more licentious than the loud Flounder-man's. (2:208 [V.v, 31–53])

And before his final defeat, Fainall, who has a legal right to his wife's goods under the law of *femme couvert*, threatens to expose his wife's body as naked as her "Reputation."[5]

The same theme of public exposure runs throughout Congreve's last three comedies. In *The Double Dealer*, for example, a play based on a situation involving that terrible moment before a marriage when, do what they will, every couple must find themselves forced to do what Millamant finds so terrible—associate with fools because they are one's relatives—Mellefont, the hero, comments on the ritual of indulging in "Tea and Scandal" (1:136 [I.i, 9–10]) after dinner. Congreve even gives us a sample of their malicious gossip as Brisk and the Froths take up Lady Toothless, who is "always chewing the Cud like an old *Yew*" (1:188 [III.x, 62]), and another person whose name Lady Froth has conveniently forgotten, identified as "the old fat Fool that Paints so exorbitantly." Brisk quickly adds, "I know whom you mean—But Deuce take me I can't hit of her Name neither—Paints d'ye say? Why she lays it on with a Trowel—Then she has a great Beard that bristles through it, and makes her look as if she were plaister'd with Lime and Hair, let me perish" (1:189 [III.x, 76–80]). Brisk, who is a pretender to wit and culture, confesses that he wrote a song on this lady, and though he was uncertain whether it was "an Epigram, or rather an Epigrammatick Sonnet," he was certain that it was "Satire" (1:189 [III.x, 84–86]).

Of course this concern with satire and lampoon may be treated as a phase of literary history, but it is apparent that the popularity of these forms was a reflection of a crisis in society at large. In *A Discourse Concerning Satire*, published in 1693, John Dryden attempted to distinguish between writers of lampoons and writers of satires, describing satire as a branch of "moral philosophy" and arguing that the best satirist was he who "instructs most usefully." The lampoon, on the other hand, was "of dangerous example to the public," because the lampooner might by "mixing sense with malice, blast the reputation of the most innocent amongst men, and the most virtuous amongst women." In his discussion of some of Horace's replies to his enemies, he added that the lampoon was "a dangerous sort of weapon, and for the most part unlawful. We have no moral right on the reputation of other men. 'Tis taking from them what we cannot restore to them." Dryden allows only two defenses for writing lampoons: revenge and a motivation that Pope would appeal to in the next century, that "'Tis an action of virtue to make examples of vicious men."[6]

The literary debate over the value of general as opposed to specific satire continued throughout the next century and received particular attention from Steele in *The Tatler*.[7] As a social phenomenon, however, the lampoon served the same function as the Black Lists of moral offenders published by the Societies for the Reformation of Manners, founded in 1692, in that they both exposed reputations to public ridicule. And however much the writers of stage comedy denied that their satire was specific, they were doing very much the same thing; this was one reason why comedy was beginning to get on people's nerves. In Thomas D'Urfey's *The Richmond Heiress*, first performed in April 1693, the cast of characters included Tom Romance, whose chief pleasure in any affair was to publish the lady's loss of virtue to all his friends, Madame Squeamish, who enters objecting to a lampoon that has been written against her, and Sophronia, a female satirist, who attacks the times in speeches criticizing the life of the town and the rule of money in society.[8] Not surprisingly, D'Urfey was continually defending his plays from the imputation of particular satire or lampoon. "Modest Reproof is taken for absurd Abuse," he complained, "and honest Satyr for Dogmatick Slaunder."[9] No sophisticated literary critic himself, D'Urfey got Charles Gildon to write a preface to one of his plays explaining that the end of comedy was "Satyr [...] since from its beginning, 'twas design'd to correct Vice, and Folly by exposing them." Such an exposure, Gildon argued, often included, as was the case with the ancient Greek playwright, Aristophanes, naming particular men and women.[10] For all Gildon's theorizing, a contemporary satire on D'Urfey introduces him as eager for news about the latest scandal and lampoon.[11] Congreve's *The Double Dealer* came under the same kind of attack as D'Urfey's comedies. "The women thinke he has exposd their Bitchery too much," wrote Dryden, "& the Gentlemen, are offended with him; for the discovery of their follyes: & the way of their Intrigues, under the notion of Friendship to their Ladyes Husbands."[12]

I want to return to this problem of public scandal and its relation to the private life later in this chapter, but it should be clear by now that I am in complete disagreement with Charles Lamb's argument, mentioned previously, to the effect that the comedies of Congreve and his contemporaries had nothing to do with the real world and should be classified with the fairy tales of the brothers Grimm and Hans Christian Andersen. Restoration comedy often presents a uniform surface, but over a period of 40 years the alterations were startling, and many of these alterations were related directly to political and social change. That Congreve borrowed more dramatic ideas and techniques from Wycherley and Dryden than from a comic realist like Thomas D'Urfey is hardly surprising, yet the plays D'Urfey wrote in the 1690s share with Congreve's plays a common spirit and subject matter. Certainly, Congreve would not have disagreed with the sentiment of two lines from D'Urfey's prologue to *The Richmond Heiress*:

> All are craz'd now—Beaux, Warriors, Citts, Projectors.
> The World's the Stage, and all Mankind are Actors.[13]

2

In what may have been his last work, his *Letter to Viscount Cobham*, Congreve warned against falling into the habit of nostalgia for former days and a too severe condemnation of the present:

> For Virtue now is neither more or less,
> And Vice is only varied in the Dress;
> Believe it, Men have ever been the same,
> And Ovid's Golden Age, is but a Dream.[14]

If we adopt Congreve's abderitic view of history, we might question some of the statements made by some modern historians about the reign of William and Mary, particularly statements about the stage of that time. David Ogg remarked, "after the Revolution, Englishmen awoke to the fact that their metropolis was one of the most disorderly and dissipated cities in Europe, and that Restoration drama was the most obscene thing of its kind in the history of literature."[15] Dudley Bahlman, in his book, *The Moral Revolution of 1688*, questions whether the numerous contemporary statements about the decay of moral standards represented anything more than a state of mind, but he does suggest one area where there was an obvious sign of moral degeneracy. "It is not difficult," he wrote, "to assess the moral laxness of the stage. The plays of Farquhar, Congreve, and Vanbrugh furnish valid evidence. For the other dangers complained of by the moralists there is no yardstick."[16] In fact, the state of mind some ten years following the Glorious Revolution represented an overreaction to the sophisticated freedoms accepted during the reigns of Charles II and James II. After Jeremy Collier's attack on the stage in 1698, actors were arrested for performing *Love for Love*, a play that by our standards might be thought of as moderately risqué.[17] There was a loud outcry about comedy being immoral and about profanity, yet in some ways the comedy of the time was intensely moral.

The fact that people felt that things had gone wrong, however, is important. James Wright attacked the vices of the city in 1693, focusing on creeping permissiveness. "The Children in the City," he wrote, "are taught to forget all that is decent in a Child, the Parents care being to bring them to a bold Confidence, which ends in the Contempt of those that begot them; and this they miscall Wit, and hopeful forwardness; they allow them to encrease in these Follies, all the criminal Liberty their Age is capable of making use of."[18] Indeed, young men known as "scourers" were outraging their elders by rioting and breaking windows, but Wright's love of the country and dislike of the city aside, what we have in complaints such as these is a feeling of discomfort in the presence of change. The revolution of 1688, once treated almost exclusively as a political phenomenon, was, of course, far broader in its implications for English society. Bahlman's book, *The Moral Revolution*, treats the changes that occurred during this period through the operations of the Society for the Propagation of Christian Knowledge and Societies for the Reformation of Manners; P. G. M. Dickson's *The Financial Revolution in England* covers the changes in banking and government financing that came about at this time, partly through the efforts of Charles Montagu, Congreve's patron; and Geoffroy Atkinson's *The Sentimental Revolution*, while it concentrates on French writers, suggests a general change in Europe's social and emotional outlook in the 1690s. And most recently, after much doubt had been heaped on the notion that very much had changed with the Glorious Revolution, Steve Pincus's *1688* has argued most forcefully that the revolution changed English politics and economic policy in startling ways.

But revolutions seldom happen without psychological hangovers. William III had rescued England from James II, absolutism, and Catholicism, but not before a three-year reign during which many Englishmen had viewed themselves surrendering their liberties without much of a struggle. The war with James and then with Louis XIV found Englishmen without an experienced army and with some self-doubts about the courage of their military leaders. Clergymen, who had preached nonresistance and passive obedience, found themselves in active rebellion against their king and their principles. Scandals centering in bribery of government officials undermined public confidence.[19]

Many politicians kept open a correspondence with the Pretender; it was a time of deception and doubt. As if this were not enough, the equivalent of a women's liberation movement, probably a product of the new leisure of the middle-class housewife and an English queen ruling equally with her husband, began to plead for rights. The entire class structure seemed to relax somewhat, opening social opportunities for merchants and tradesmen that were not possible before.[20] In 1690, John Locke had offered readers a new epistemology; John Norris and Richard Burthogge were soon countering with mystical systems; Thomas Burnet's theories about paradise were shocking people even more than his ideas on Noah's Flood; and deists like Charles Blount and John Toland were becoming more outspoken. To complicate matters, a great deal of attention was being paid to the beaux, a word first used, according to the *OED*, in 1687, to describe men who paid an inordinate attention to appearance and manners, while the wits had practically incorporated themselves into a faction.[21] Swift, who began his *Tale of a Tub* during this period, viewed this complex of wits, beaux, philosophers, and heretics as a single entity, the main features of which were emptiness and irrationality. But for others the times must have seemed exciting. There was a new sophistication about art, literature, and philosophy. Motteux's *Gentleman's Journal*, started in 1692, provided a periodical in which one might come on a new song by Congreve set to music by Purcell or Eccles, a translation of one of Horace's odes, a novella, a review of the latest play, a discussion of the theories of Descartes or Malebranche, or some comments on the neglect of women in English society. If some saw signs that the end of the world was near, others must have felt the Enlightenment just around the corner.

3

Writers like Congreve, Southerne, and Vanbrugh aimed their comedies at the audience that read *The Gentleman's Journal*, an audience that wanted entertainment but also liked serious dialogue on contemporary problems. As a result, the critical center of Restoration comedy shifted drastically in the direction of dialogue. As early as 1686, D'Urfey was complaining of the need to "adapt [...] Scenes and Story to the Genius of the Critick," who was no longer being pleased by "Humour" or "Plot."[22] And six years later, in his preface to D'Urfey's *The Marriage Hater Match'd*, Charles Gildon was defending D'Urfey's style of comedy (Dryden called it farce) against the "Bundle of Dialogues" employed by writers like Congreve. Gildon's remark that Terence "took care of Plot as well as words" is interesting here in view of its obvious appeal to Terence's high reputation as a writer whose comedies tended to avoid farcical scenes and present a realistic view of society.[23]

Most writers of comedy, however, had not advanced to the critical position of Addison, who in his *Spectator* essay of October 6, 1712, was to praise Terence's *Self-Tormentor* for its "sober and polite Mirth," there not being in it "one passage that could raise a laugh." Congreve, Southerne, and Vanbrugh, the best representatives of the new comic mode, were all interested in raising laughs, and they used a tried comic formula for just that purpose. John Phillips, the supposed author of *Reflection on Our Modern Poesy* (1695), gave a satirical description of that formula in the following manner:

> His Gentlemen he makes a Wondrous Sage,
> That's deeply read in Vices of the Age:
> His Mistress and his Cloaths employ his Care;
> Of all his Thoughts his Country claims no share.
> The Damsel too, e'er Fifteen Years expire,
> Is all o'er Love, and wanton with Desire;
> And nought will please her, but the Name of Bride:
> Which once obtain'd does soon uneasie prove,
> And still she trafficks in Forbidden Love;
> Her Husband's Kisses lose their wonted Taste,
> And stollen Pleasures always Relish best.[24]

Were it possible to neutralize the ironic tone of these lines, most of the writers of comedy would have had no difficulty recognizing in this description an approximation of their heroes and heroines. They might even have agreed with Phillips's statement that comedy should be a "Glass, where all might see / How to correct their own Deformity." But they would not have accepted his ideas on the means by which this was to be achieved:

> And though the Age's Humour he expose,
> Yet no Unseemly things should he disclose.[25]

How, they would have asked, is one to show deformity unless one shows what is unseemly? If the stage is a glass, Vanbrugh argued, "People ought therefore to see themselves as they are."[26] And Congreve insisted that by its very nature comedy must show "vicious Characters" behaving themselves "foolishly, or immorally in Word or Deed."[27] They did not object to the idea of functioning as moralists, but they insisted that as such they had to write as satiric realists. The names of Aristophanes, Rabelais, and Cervantes, the masters of realistic satire, are repeatedly invoked within the plays and in prefaces, prologues, and epilogues, and the lengthy catalogues and realistic detail in Congreve's comedies probably owe something to the vogue of these writers.

The important point, however, is that although clergymen like Jeremy Collier and Arthur Bedford shared with the comic playwrights something of the new seriousness toward manners and morals, their approach to such problems was very different. The former saw the theater in competition with religion, the church, and the clergy. They wanted to close the theaters; the latter thought in terms of comedy as a moral form. When Vanbrugh said of the conflict between himself and Collier, "I almost fancy when He and I are fast asleep in our Graves, those who shall read what we both have produc'd will be apt to conclude there's a Mistake in the Tradition about the Authors; and that 'twas the Reforming Divine writ the Play, and the Scandalous Poet the Remarks upon't,"[28] unless he was thinking forward to the second half of the twentieth century, he was not only overly optimistic about the future relationship of art to its audience but also wrong about his role. Like Congreve, Vanbrugh was a moralist only as a writer of brilliant social comedy is a moralist. The thought that anyone might think *The Relapse* was written by a clergyman reveals the degree to which writers can misconceive the nature of moral statement in their art. On the other hand, if Congreve and Vanbrugh believed they were using their artistry to make serious ethical statements, they were certainly right. I will examine this problem at further length both in this chapter and throughout this book.

4

Before proceeding to some specific remarks on Congreve's comedies in relation to this moral milieu, I would like to glance at a few contemporary comedies by minor writers, since it is in such works that normative trends will appear, uncontaminated by any signs of original genius. A good example for my purposes is a play by Thomas Wright, *The Female Vertuoso's*, produced in 1693. In his dedication, Wright states that he wanted to write satirically and took, "besides some modern Poets, Aristophanes for a Pattern," though he questioned whether this would please the audience. "We are grown Serious," he remarked, "and cannot relish Fooleries."[29] The play opens with the news that a city mob, which has set itself up as a vigilante group to punish vice, has just beaten up a country gentleman, Sir Timothy Witless, one of the many fools in the play. But this proves to be merely a bit of contemporary setting as the play turns to the central problem of how Sir Maurice, a London merchant, will be able to gain sufficient courage to cope with his dominating wife, Lady Meanwell, who spends her time either reading romances or engaging in a variety of mad projects. Lady Meanwell is a product of the new leisure that came to middle-class wives as a result of an increase in servants and in services offered by city shopkeepers.[30] Sir Maurice complains,

> I am no Scholar, not I, and I thank my Stars for it, but with your leave so much common Sense has taught me, that all the Study and Philosophy of a Wife, should be to please her Husband, instruct her Children, have a Vigilant Eye over Domestick Affairs, keep a good Order in her Family, and stand as a Living Pattern of Virtue, and Discretion to all about her [...] The Women of Old did not read so much, but lived better, Housewifry was all the Knowledge they aspired to [...] I will have a Reformation in my House [...] This Plague of Wit has infected all my Servants, even my little Boy, forsooth, cannot turn the Spit now without Pharamond, or a Cassandra in his hand; if I call for Drink, the Butler brings me a Spencer, or Ben Johnson.[31]

Sir Maurice's crisis of courage may have been symbolic of the contemporary experience of the English male on both a domestic and national level. All of Europe was experiencing a legal and moral crisis over marriage, and however wry might be the advice of Sir Timothy to his son, Witless, on the subject of his future wife's virtue, it was certainly not impractical. "Cuckoldam," states Sir Timothy in telling his son to accept his fate, "is a raging Grievance of the Nation [...] Just now, believe me, as many men as you see walking in the Streets, are as many Cuckolds."[32] In spite of this assertion, the traditional young comic hero, Clerimont, is deeply in love with the heroine, Mariana, and is willing to marry her, even without a dowry. He tells Sir Maurice, "As it was not for her Fortune I courted your fair Daughter, so this Loss shall make no change in me; I love her better than ever I did, all I have in the World is hers, and consequently at your service."[33] The play ends happily enough for a comedy of the time—not with the reformation of Sir Maurice's wife but with a separation of the older couple and the marriage of the young.

This play and many others written at the time show that the writers of comedy shared many of the moral concerns of those crying for a reformation of manners. The comedies still involved cuckolding and love affairs, but the emotional center became a marriage for love. If the young hero was still the sexually experienced male, he was now capable of genuine affection and true love. Clerimont's profession of love was typical for this period. Blunt, in Shadwell's comedy *The Volunteers* (1692), maintains, "I never knew a Valiant fellow, but he was Amourous and Compassionate, nor a Coward, but he was Cruel and Lustful."[34] Lord Worthy, in William Mountfort's *Greenwich-Park* (1692), falls in love at first sight and tells the somewhat skeptical lady he is wooing,

> Love, as it's unaccountable, is irresistable.
> There must be a beginning, why not now?

A Laziness in liking is insipid.
Nor would you prize the lightning of your Eyes,
If it were slow in giving us the Wound.
That flint is best, that fires at first stroak.[35]

The ideal hero of the 1690s was to combine genuine feeling with a certain grace. As Eugenia says in Shadwell's *The Scourers* (1690), "When a man is lewd with a bon Grace there's something in it; but a Fellow that is aukwardly wicked is not to be born."[36] He was to combine a stoic restraint with an epicurean ease. A hero like Bellamy, in Shadwell's *Bury Fair* (1689), who announces, "He that Debauches private Women, is a Knave, and injures others: And he that uses publick ones, is a Fool and hurts himself."[37] Shadwell's Bellamy might seem uncommonly priggish, but the ideal of the time did turn toward a hero capable of true love.

Few writers, however, were willing to settle for sentimental clichés, and if they showed a couple capable of love and marriage, they usually surrounded them with a gallery of fools and knaves. George Powell's *A Very Good Wife* (1693), for which Congreve wrote a prologue, shows one such couple surviving all the adversity that a venal and vicious society can provide. The hero, Courtwit, succeeds in recovering his lost money by assuming disguises that enable him to trick all those people who had taken his money and now refused to pay it back. Deceit and disguise are presented as the only way to survive, and Courtwit's final statement might have come out of that apocalyptic vision of human evil, Gracián's *El Criticón*:

In short, the whole false World is all Deceit,
And I've made bold ev'n to retrieve the Cheat,
Think not of Losses. Therefore where there's none,
For all my Care was but to get my own.[38]

Private love might well seem the only hope in a world in which, as Powell's Mrs. Sneaksby points out, honesty will get one nowhere. "What shou'd anyone Man do with Honesty," she asks, "when 'tis enough to undoe a whole Corporation."[39]

Yet in 1702, Ramble, a character in the anonymous dialogue, *A Comparison between the Two Stages*, could find the title, *A Very Good Wife*, "almost a Solaecism."[40] And the author of *The Folly of Love*, published in 1693, stated the case against marriage as clearly as most:

Of all the Plagues attending human Life,
The greatest sure is what we call a Wife;

> Nor is there a more pitied Wretch than he,
> That's doom'd to Matrimonial Slavery.[41]

Even works sympathetic to women, such as William Walsh's *A Dialogue Concerning Women, Being a Defence of the Sex* (1691), couched its "Defence" in the skeptical dialogue form with replies to questions such as why women do not cuckold their husbands with men of sense rather than with fools, or why women always "inveigh against the Lampooners, and at the same time talk as scandalously as they can write."[42] With questions of this sort, the battle is half lost before it can begin. Even the feminist Mary Astell attacked women for their self-love, and one of the more exciting questions of the time was whether men or women were more dominated by that central human quality.[43]

On the general question of the relation of the sexes, it was a time of open argument and debate. Such a situation could produce brilliant plays like Southerne's *Cuckolds Make Themselves* (1691) or jumbles like Crowne's *The Married Beau* (1694). Crowne's play is a good example of what happened to the stuff of late Restoration comedy in the hands of a lesser craftsman. *The Married Beau* is an adaptation of Cervantes's brilliant novella "The Curious Impertinent," from *Don Quixote*, in which a man asks his best friend to test the virtue of his wife. She yields to temptation, and after an initial period in which the husband is deceived, the story ends sadly with the deaths of the three characters, the husband of embarrassment, the wife of shame, and the lover in a fight. In Crowne's hands, the story ends happily enough. The husband, Mr. Lovely, as the title would suggest, is a beau, a man suffering from self-love and therefore incapable of giving real love. He wants to be certain that his wife loves him completely—that he has her "soul." When his friend lies to him and informs him that his wife is innocent and in love with her husband, he plans an orgy that combines sexual pleasure with self-love:

> My luxury will consist in curiosity.
> My eyes shall wander o'er her face to spy
> If, when I kiss her, she's entranc'd with joy.[44]

Although his wife has indeed been seduced, the play ends with the deceived beau expressing his happiness at his wife's love for him.

The bulk of the play, however, is taken up with discussions of love, the social and legal position of women, and what the beau calls "the spreading heresy, / That nature is the same in all mankind, / And lewd in all."[45] Nothing is ever resolved except that some men are happier living with their illusions. And this type of inconclusiveness was symptomatic of the plays of the time. The total effect is not so much satire as that quality that Saint-Evremond praised in Petronius, whom he saw as an author lacking the qualities of a Horace, "a publick Censurer, that makes it his Business to expose Corruptions," but having rather the politeness and wit of a gentleman and courtier who "turns everything into Ridicule."[46]

Notes

1 John Dryden, *Works*, ed. H. T. Swedenberg et al., 20 vols. (Berkeley: University of California Press, 1956–2000), 4:433.
2 Charles Lamb, "On the Artificial Comedy of the Last Century," *Complete Works and Letters of Charles Lamb* (New York: Modern Library, 1935), 108.
3 William Congreve, *The Works of William Congreve*, ed. D. F. McKenzie and C. Y. Ferdinand, 3 vols. (Oxford: Oxford University Press, 2011), 2:106 (I.i, 49–50). All subsequent citations to Congreve's writings will refer to this edition and be placed within parentheses in my text.
4 *Journals of the House of Lords* (n.p., n.d.), XV, 340, 37, 42, 46–47, et passim. See also Narcissus Luttrell, *A Brief Relation of State Affairs* (Oxford: University Press, 1857), 1:358–359; 2:342, 362; and Gellert Alleman, *Matrimonial Law in Restoration Comedy* (Philadelphia, PA: Wallingford, 1942), 135–41.
5 For an excellent, brief discussion of the legal rights of married women to property, see David Ogg, *England in the Reigns of James II and William III* (Oxford: Clarendon Press, 1966), 77–78. For a more complicated and thorough examination of the problem, see Susan Staves, *Married Women's Separate Property in England, 1660–1833* (Cambridge: Harvard University Press, 1990), especially 130–95.
6 *A Discourse Concerning the Original and Progress of Satire*, in *Of Dramatic Poesy and Other Critical Essays*, ed. George Watson (London: Dent, 1962), 2:78, 122, 125–26.
7 See, e.g., numbers 41, 76, 92, 242.
8 For some sense of the satire in these comedies, compare the similarity in tone between the speech in which Sophronia remarks, "Money is now the Soul o'th'Universe" (*The Richmond Heiress* [London, 1693, 45]), and formal satires such as Robert Gould's "The Corruption of the Times by Money" (1693), in *Works* (London, 1709), 2:263–297.
9 *The Marriage Hater Match'd* (London, 1692), sig. A2v.
10 Ibid., sigs. A1–a1. Gildon appealed to the practice of Aristophanes, whose reputation improved as writers sought justification for specific satire.
11 *Wit for Money: or, Poet Stutter* (London, 1692), sig. A2v. There is a similar picture of D'Urfey in *Poeta Infamis: Or, a Poet Not Worth Hanging* (London, 1692), 9.
12 John Dryden, *Letters*, ed. Charles Wald (New York: AMS Press, 1965), 63.
13 D'Urfey, *The Richmond Heiress*, sig. A3v.
14 William Congreve, *Complete Works*, ed. D. F. McKenzie and C. Y. Ferdinand, 3 vols. (Oxford: Oxford University Press, 2011), 2:488.
15 *England in the Reigns of lames II and William III*, 530.
16 Dudley Bahlman, *The Moral Revolution of 1688* (New Haven: Yale University Press, 1957), 6.
17 See Arthur Bedford, *The Evil and Danger of Stage Plays* (London, 1706), 4, 223.
18 *The Humours, and Conversations of the Town* (London, 1693), 20.
19 See Thomas Dilke, *The Lover's Luck* (London, 1696), 24, for a comment on the "late Briberies" and the conclusion that "private interest in Persons of Trust never fails

to over-ballance the publick Concern." For a comment on the clergy, see William Mountfort, *Greenwich-Park* (London, 1691), 3.
20. The new social mobility is frequently commented upon in contemporary comedies. In John Crowne's *The English Friar* (London, 1690), Lord Stately is satirized for his nostalgia about the class distinctions of the past, and the serious heroine, Julia, argues (85) that "manners" are more important than either wealth or title.
21. For some typical comments on wits and beaus, see Peter Motteux, *Love's a Jest* (Buck, 1696), 3–10.
22. Thomas D'Urfey, *The Banditti* (London, 1686), sig. a4.
23. Sigs. A4–A4 v. In *Poeta Infamis*, 11, D'Urfey defends his dramatic practice by a reference to "my Master Terence."
24. John Phillips, *Reflection on Our Modern Poesy* (London, 1695), 5.
25. Ibid.
26. John Vanbrugh, *A Short Vindication of the Relapse and Provok'd Wife*, in *Complete Works*, ed. Bonamy Dobrée and Geoffrey Webb, 4 vols. (London: Nonesuch, 1927), 1:206.
27. Congreve, *Complete Works*, 3:78.
28. Vanbrugh, *Short Vindication*, 1:214.
29. Thomas Wright, *The Female Vertuoso's* (London, 1693), sig. A2v.
30. For a useful discussion of this general change in English society, see Ian Watt, *The Rise of the Novel* (Berkeley: University of California Press, 1959), 44–46.
31. Wright, *The Female Vertuoso's*, 25–26.
32. Ibid., 47.
33. Ibid., 48.
34. *Works*, ed. Montague Summers, 5 vols. (London: Fortune Press, 1927), 5:180.
35. William Mountfort, *Greenwich-Park* (London, 1691), 19.
36. Shadwell, *Works*, 5:97.
37. Ibid., 4:309.
38. George Powell, *A Very Good Wife* (London, 1693), 47.
39. Ibid., 4.
40. Staring B. Wells, ed., *A Comparison between the Two Stages* (Princeton, NJ: Princeton University Press, 1942), 16.
41. Robert Gould, *The Folly of Love. A New Satyr against Women*, 2nd ed. (London, 1693), 14.
42. William Walsh, *A Dialogue Concerning Women, Being a Defence of the Sex* (London: 1691), 14, 29, 66–71.
43. Mary Astell, *A Farther Essay Relating to the Female-Sex* (London, 1696), 73–103.
44. John Crowne, *The Married Beau: or, The Curious Impertinent*, in *Dramatic Works*, ed. James Maidment and W. H. Logan, 5 vols. (Edinburgh: W. Patterson, 1874), 4:316.
45. Crowne, *The Married Beau, Dramatic Works*, 4:261 (II.i).
46. Charles de Saint-Evremond, *Works* (London, 1700), 1:223.

Figure 2 Details. Richard van Bleeck's *Portrait of Congreve*. Leuven, Stedjick Museum. (a) Vanbrugh's *The Provoked Wife*. (b) Volume of the Philosopher George Berkeley.

Chapter 2

INCOGNITA AND SOME PROBLEMS IN MORALITY AND EPISTEMOLOGY

The serious subject matter of a play such as Crowne's *The Married Beau*, discussed in the previous chapter, returns us to Vanbrugh's claim to being a "moralist" and the possibility of stage comedies being vehicles for moral statement. Although such a proposition might appear inane enough to any generation that lived to see the comedies of George Bernard Shaw and Bertholt Brecht, it did not seem at all evident to Jeremy Collier in 1698. As I remarked, my approach to Congreve's plays in this volume is through the ideas they convey, broadly philosophical, political, and social. I have no intention of denying that Congreve was eminently a man of the theater. His involvement with Thomas Betterton in listening to readings of the plays performed at the Lincoln Inn Fields theater shows how much he was involved with the intricacies or theatrical representation.[1] Nevertheless, when dealing with a writer such as Congreve, it is necessary to discard the approach to Restoration drama of Robert Hume, who pointedly ignores an intellectual approach to drama as almost irrelevant.[2] A time of political and intellectual strife, the last 40 years of the seventeenth century may well have been best summarized by Jonathan Swift's *Tale of a Tub* with its whirlwind of ideas on philosophical and religious beliefs—beliefs that led its readers into such complete confusion that insanity might seem a possible way out. Similarly, in matters of politics, many English men and English women, including such writers as John Dryden, Aphra Behn, and Thomas Southerne, remained loyal to the deposed king, James II, and a system of monarchy that gave him complete control over the lives of his subjects. On the other hand, Congreve was seriously committed to the politics surrounding the Glorious Revolution of 1688, the regimes of William and Mary and then of William III. And as his writings reveal, he appears to have been equally committed to the philosophical empiricism of the time, from René Descartes to George Berkeley—a view that acknowledged that we know the world only through our perception of it through our senses. He may have held such a view before the publication of John Locke's *Essay Concerning Human Understanding* (1690), but it is also true that his "novel," *Incognita* (1691), with its confusion of persons, names, and identities, is open to interpretation through a reading of Locke's work, not as a direct influence but as a work offering a mirror reflecting some of the ideas of the time.[3]

1

I will return to this problem of names and identities later in this chapter in treating Congreve's "novel," *Incognita*, but before such a discussion, and before I want to be seen as applying a heavy-handed approach to someone often thought as a writer of fairly frivolous comedies, I want to examine an excellent essay by D. F. McKenzie, written shortly before his death, titled "Richard Van Bleeck's Painting of William Congreve as Contemplative" (1715). The essay involves the analysis of a portrait of the playwright when he was in his 47th year. He was having severe difficulties with his vision and his eyelids appear heavy. His hand is open to a volume of Vanbrugh's *The Provoked Wife*, with an allusion to another play by Vanbrugh, *The Relapse*. His right arm rests upon a pile of books, one of which is identified as being by the philosopher George Berkeley. There is a pocket watch on the table that appears to allude to time itself. McKenzie quotes approvingly from an essay treating the artist and this particular portrait, describing Congreve in terms of "cette effige pensive et noble," and he follows this by remarking, "Van Bleeck's painting is unequivocally Philosophical."[4]

McKenzie has no difficulty associating the painted volume of Berkeley's philosophy with the philosophy of some passages of Congreve's tragedy, *The Mourning Bride*, but he treats the allusion to Vanbrugh's relationship with Congreve as mainly involved in the theater, particularly in 1704 and 1705, when they collaborated on *Squire Trelooby*, were selected by Queen Anne as involved in overseeing the morality of theatrical productions, and worked together on the new theater in the Haymarket. Although all of these relationships could explain why Congreve might have paid Vanbrugh this compliment, they certainly do not explain why he would have introduced this allusion to his friend in a painting that was "unequivocally Philosophical." It would seem that Congreve was making a statement about the nature of the two plays by Vanbrugh that appear in Van Bleeck's painting. We should recall once more Vanbrugh's response to Collier to the effect that, lacking a background into Collier's attack, future readers of these plays and Collier's attack upon them might be more likely to decide that the playwright was the moralist and the clergyman was the playwright. If in my introductory chapter I had argued for a degree of absurdity in Vanbrugh's position, this does not mean that both Vanbrugh and Congreve failed to consider their comedies serious ethical works.

In writing *The Relapse* (1696), Vanbrugh was replying to Colley Cibber's play *Love's Last Shift* (1696) in which the character of Loveless has absented himself from his wife, Amanda, for 10 years, and returns to England with the notion that his wife is dead. He succeeds in seducing Amanda, whom he does not recognize. She reveals her identity and Loveless repents. There are certainly some amusing comic moments: Cibber, as Sir Novelty Fashion, must have been extremely funny. The play is sometimes treated as the first sentimental comedy. But what is most important is the presentation of a coarse notion of sex. The conversion of Loveless in Cibber's play must have been satisfying to some of the audience, but, as sometimes with later sentimental comedy, the ideas are essentially unexamined. The fact that Amanda brings a fortune with her to the penniless Loveless does not lend confidence to his conversion. The rape of Amanda's maid by Snap, while his master is having intercourse with her mistress is not particularly comforting, and the epilogue points out that the morality of the play is hardly believable. Vanbrugh was clearly not convinced. He would probably have joined with Bernard Mandeville a few years later when Mandeville commented on the Third Earl of Shaftesbury's belief in the essential goodness of human beings—it was a lovely notion, what a shame it was not true.[5]

Most of all, Vanbrugh approached human relationships from a variety of standpoints, raising numerous ethical points while allowing the dialogic elements of the drama to enable his audience to consider the possibilities permitted to human experience. It should be noted that all of this occurs in plays that are remarkably funny. The scene of Sir Lord Foppington's descent upon the country estate of Sir Tunbelly Clumsy to marry the insanely sensual if "innocent" Hoyden, his treatment as an impostor by the servants, and his ending up in the dog kennel in *The Relapse,* and Sir John Brute before the law for drunken and riotous behavior when dressed as a parson (or even more amusing in the later version when dressed as a woman) in *The Provoked Wife* have more pure comic spirit than anything in Congreve. But in the midst of this laughter, Vanbrugh has his audience listen to versions of behavior that extend from the carefree sensuality of Mademoiselle, the maid of Lady Fanciful, to the stoic virtue of Amanda, pursuing virtue for its own reward. The virtue of Amanda is borrowed from Colley Cibber's *Love's Last Shift.* Vanbrugh does not dismiss it entirely; in the end, it is praised by Worthy, who appears, at first, to have little concern with anything but his pleasure.

Like Congreve's *Love for Love*, Vanbrugh's *Relapse* begins with Loveless reading Stoic philosophy. He swears his fidelity to his wife, Amanda, and he is faithful so long as he is able to follow his reason. Unfortunately for his resolve to follow a rational life, he quickly succumbs to the passions, which Vanbrugh, like most of his contemporaries, believed to be the governing principles of human kind. Hence the inevitable "relapse" and the answer to Cibber's simplistic presentation of human nature in *Love's Last Shift.* With the introduction of Berinthia, the friend of Amanda who will betray her by allowing Loveless, Amanda's husband, to seduce her, Vanbrugh interjects a serious discussion of the nature of men and women, of love, and of marriage. Berinthia starts her conversation with Amanda by pointing out the difference between the beaux, fops, and those men who are worthy of consideration. The first group is governed by self-love; the second may be governed by their passions, but they are considerate of those whom they love. She deceives Amanda, and at one point praises intrigue as using all of a woman's faculties: "Hypocrisy, Invention, Deceit, Flattery, Mischief, and Lying."[6] Compared with the naiveté of Amanda, Berinthia's view of the world is refreshing.

When she gets together with Worthy, her former lover, the couple in some ways seem much like Valmont and the Marquise de Merteuil in Laclos's *Liaisons Dangereuses*. Both couples possess knowledge of the ways of the world. And they both are out to seduce two well-meaning people. But from the very beginning of their correspondence, Valmont and Merteuil reveal an only partially submerged antagonism. Berinthia and Worthy are friends who share a common attitude toward the pleasures of the world. They do not see themselves as hurting Loveless and Amanda in any way. "If you follow as you shou'd do (my dear Berinthia)," says Worthy, "we may all four pass the winter very pleasantly."[7] Of course, Amanda is indeed left unhappy at the end with the knowledge of her husband's betrayal, but she ultimately has her triumph. "Yet still the Sovereignty is in the Mind," she tells Worthy, "whene'er it pleases to exert its force."[8] Worthy admits that the "Robe of Virtue" can be a "graceful Habit." He still holds on to the idea that virtue is something that may be put on and off, but Amanda wins in the end, at least on her own terms.[9]

There is considerable discussion about marriage in *The Relapse*, particularly between Amanda and Berinthia, but the broader theme of relationships, including everything from sex to friendship, composes the intellectual basis of *The Provoked Wife*. We open with Sir John Brute's complaint: "What cloying Meat is Love—When Matrimony's the Sauce to it! Two Years Marriage has debauch my five Senses. Every thing I see, every thing I hear, every thing I feel, every thing I smell, and ever thing I taste—methinks has Wife in it."[10] He admits that there is nothing wrong with his wife, but he simply cannot stand her. He married her for "Love," but that has evaporated. She married him for his money and position, but the benefits of those have proved illusory. This is followed by a conversation between Lady Brute and her sister-in-law, Belinda, in which the latter confesses her weakness for Constant. Lady Brute advises a degree of self-control over the "Body's Weakness." This is followed by a discourse between Lady Fanciful and her French maid, Madamoiselle. Lady Fanciful is shocked by her maid's advocacy of free sexuality: "Je suis Philosophe," she states, and when Lady Fanciful expresses disbelief that she would sacrifice her honor to her pleasure, Mademoiselle argues for following nature rather than reason.[11]

In the second act, we have Sir John explaining how he got into the marriage he now regrets. The present Lady Brute would not let him have sexual intercourse with her, so he achieved his goal through marriage. He hates all women except the whores with whom he was involved on the previous night. We are also introduced to Heartfree and Constant, two men who profess Libertine principles. They mock concepts of chastity as foolish conventions. Lady Brute is attracted to Constant and Bellinda to Heartfree. The two Libertines find themselves reluctantly attracted to the women. Bellinda decides she is willing to marry Heartfree despite his poverty. She is ready to marry for love, though she might not do so were she so poor as to end up "in a Cell" living on "Love and Bread and Butter."[12] Sir John agrees to separate from his wife, who appears ready to accept Constant as her lover.

While it might be somewhat inaccurate to regard these plays as moral dialogues, among the subjects that receive serious and extensive consideration are the nature of good and evil, moral choice, the relationship between reason and passion, and a critique of the rules of society that make marriage a permanent legal and religious condition. If Vanbrugh appears to allow considerable leeway to a variety of positions, it might be pointed out that in his treatise on the *Law of Nature*, Vanbrugh's contemporary, Samuel Pufendorf, had provided over thirty-five folio pages toward considering marriage customs around the world in an effort to arrive at a single "natural law" governing this subject. He never came to a successful conclusion, but at a time when natural law was considered a genuine key to human behavior, he more than opened up the subject for examination.[13]

My main point is that in juxtaposing two of Vanbrugh's comedies with a philosopher who treated the nature of the human mind and perception, Congreve was not asking Van Bleeck to paint himself engaged in two different activities—allusions to reading plays and reading philosophy—but rather to Vanbrugh as an ethical thinker alongside the philosopher who, by 1715, when the painting was executed, had become famous for arguing that our ideas are perceived in and through the mind of God and that existence itself was equivalent to being perceived. Vanbrugh did not engage his audience in epistemological problems, but raised significant questions about the ethical difficulties that men and women face in attempting to deal with each other, especially when such relationships are complicated by sexual desire. That such a subject description might fit the definition of "philosophy" in the *Oxford English Dictionary* (meaning 3) will probably not make Vanbrugh into a philosopher by most modern definitions, but it appeared good enough to satisfy Congreve, who may well have been alluding to Vanbrugh's reply to Jeremy Collier by defending himself as more of a moralist than the clergyman who attacked him so severely.

2

I want to turn now to the subject I broached in my Introduction—the overall decline in Congreve's reputation. In his *Life of Garrick* (1780), Thomas Davies remarked on the seeming unwillingness to perform Congreve's plays more often. The reason for this state of affairs had little to do with the artistic nature of these works or their ability to please an audience. The reason had everything to do with the supposed immorality of his plays. Davies argued,

> I have no doubt but that had Mr. Sheridan, by his [Garrick's] advice, made some judicious alterations in Congreve's Old Batchelor, Love for Love, and the Way of the World. By retrenching some licentious expressions, and connection by some slight additions, character and sentiment, he has saved those excellent plays from oblivion, which the extreme delicacy of a refined age, whose ears are become exceedingly chaste, could not endure. Would any body believe that the song of a Soldier and Sailor was too gross for the squeamish stomachs of a whist-club? The Relapse was certainly too gross for any civilized audience, has been altered by the same hand to the Trip to Scarborough, and is now a very pleasing comedy.[14]

The only play of Congreve that was performed with some regularity in 1780 was *The Mourning Bride*, and that play was under attack for elements that were considered grotesque. It held the stage because the role of Zara was a great stage vehicle for Mrs. Siddons and other actresses of the time.

Taking out a few lines that offended the delicacy of the audience as Davies suggested, however, would hardly have been sufficient. As I remarked in an essay some time ago, by the middle of the century Congreve had replaced the Earl of Rochester as the quintessential libertine.[15] For example, a somewhat ineffectual libertine named Ranger, in Benjamin Hoadly's *The Suspicious Husband*, wanders through the play reciting verses from Congreve. The verses identify him immediately as sexually promiscuous and lacking in the proper sensibility of those male characters in the play who understand the proper relationship between men and women.

Such a view of Congreve appears relatively early. The anonymous author of *The Tryal of Skill* (1704) has Apollo warning Congreve:

> But never pretend to be Modest or Chast,
> *Th'Old Batchelor* speaks you Obscene,
> And *Love for Love* shews, notwithstanding your hast,
> That your Thoughts are Impure and Unclean.

> That meaning's Lascivious your Dialogues bear,
> Fit to grace the foul Language of *Stews*,
> And though you are said to make a Wife of a Play'r,
> You in those make a Whore of your Muse.[16]

Similarly, Edmund Burke, in a journal named *The Reformer* (1748), complained of the "Obscenity" of his plays, "as none can, without the greatest Danger to Virtue, listen to; the very texture and groundwork of some of his Plays is Lewdness, which poisons the surer, as it is set off with the Advantage of his wit." Burke complains that Congreve accepted the evil manners of his age and that in *Love for Love* the character of Angelica was "scarce consistent with any *Male*, much less *Female* Modesty."[17]

Such an attitude toward Congreve still imbues Samuel Johnson's account of Congreve in his account of the playwright in *The Lives of the Poets*. Johnson blamed what he considered to be the excessive liberty of the stage to its complete closure during the interregnum under the influence of the Puritans, and Johnson ascribed Jeremy Collier's attack on the playwrights and upon the stage in general to "religious zeal and honest indignation," arguing that some of the passages that appeared in Collier's *Short View* created a sense of "horrour" in its readers. He saw Collier's attack as a kind of awakening: "the wise and the pious caught the alarm; and the nation wondered why it had so long suffered irreligion and licentiousness to be openly taught at the publick charge."[18] Johnson rightly saw the problem for anyone attempting a response to Collier as insurmountable, though not for the entirely right reason. Johnson framed the case as a battle between religion and irreligion, whether references to religion ought to be allowed in comedy, whereas the question for Collier was whether the stage should be permitted to involve itself in religion at all or indeed should be allowed to exist at all in a Christian nation. Johnson quoted a passage from Congreve's *Love for Love* in which Sampson's pulling down the temple of Dagon becomes part of a witty exchange between Angelica and Sir Sampson Legend. The problem with the passage has nothing to do with a lack of morality or a mocking of the Old Testament. But Johnson condemned it by saying, "Here you have the sacred history burlesqued; and Sampson once more brought into the house of Dagon, to make sport for the Philistines!"[19]

As I have been arguing, the real problem was the nature of the stage itself during the 1690s. The stage had taken to putting on comedies that broached serious themes. And in so doing it was not unusual for the playwrights to make allusions to scripture. But scripture was the province of the Church of England and its weekly sermons throughout the land. Any allusion to scripture at all on the contemporary stage was to be considered blasphemous. Although Johnson distinguishes between the attack on the stage made by

William Prynne in his *Historiomastix* of 1632 and Collier's of 1698, he does so on the grounds that Collier was a member of the highest of the "High" Church of England—one of those "Non-Jurors" who had refused to sign the oaths of loyalty to William and Mary. This argument is hardly convincing.[20] In fact, the 1690s had seen a revival of "puritanism" in the form of the Society for Reformation of Manners, which enforced "blue" laws upon the citizenry, particularly upon the poorest. And the stage had been under criticism from moralists such as Thomas Wright and others several years before Collier made his attack. Merely alluding to a piece of scripture was to bring Sampson out again in the arena among the "Philistines"—out again among a secular audience seeking amusement.

Johnson saw Congreve as among those who attempted futilely to fight against Collier:

> Congreve, a very young man, elated with success, and impatient of censure, assumed an air of confidence and security. His chief artifice of controversy is to retort upon his adversary his own words: he is very angry, and, hoping to conquer Collier with his own weapons, allows himself in the use of every term of contumely and contempt; but he has the sword without the arm of Scanderbeg; he has his antagonist's coarseness, but not his strength. Collier replied; for contest was his delight: he was not to be frighted from his purpose or his prey.
>
> The cause of Congreve was not tenable: whatever glosses he might use for the defence or palliation of single passages, the general tenour and tendency of his plays must always be condemned. It is acknowledged, with universal conviction, that the perusal of his works will make no man better; and that their ultimate effect is to represent pleasure in alliance with vice, and to relax those obligations by which life ought to be regulated.[21]

Johnson gets most things wrong. Certainly nothing in Congreve's comedies tends to "relax those obligations by which life ought to be regulated," unless he means, among other things, that women should stay content in marriages, which bring them nothing but misery or that children should be forced to obey tyrannical fathers. But it demonstrates why Davies's suggestion about attempting to revive somewhat "improved" versions of Congreve could not be easily done during the second half of the eighteenth century. Congreve's name had become synonymous with blasphemy and immorality. As Johnson remarks, the stage was "publick." An audience had to pay to see works performed. Following Collier's attack, there were frequent complaints in the prologues of the time about the scant audiences attending plays. In addition, actors were harassed by grand juries.[22] The comedies of Congreve and some of his fellow playwrights were revised in such a way as to remove the offending lines, and the theater gradually became respectable enough to regain its audience.[23] But Congreve's name became synonymous with the libertinism that had flourished during the Restoration.

As I will attempt to show in my discussion of *The Way of the World*, Congreve's reply to Collier was essentially political rather than either aesthetic, moral, or religious. Congreve has become the leading defender of the reigns of William and Mary and then of William III. His literary reputation as both a playwright and a poet gave particular status to his poetry in behalf of the regime. These included poems in praise of William such as *The Birth of the Muse*, a poem mourning the death of Queen Mary, and a description of William's victory at the battle of Namur. Collier's stance as a nonjuror made him an enemy of William, and he was to appear notoriously on the scaffold of those assassinated for an attempted assassination of the monarch. Collier appears in Congreve's *Amendments of Collier's False and Imperfect Citations* (1698) as a traitor to the state, a clergyman who would not acknowledge the monarch of his country, and as a modern Guy Fawkes, whose attempt to destroy the stage was equivalent to the plot of Guy Fawkes to blow up the state.

Congreve was hardly the only one who replied to Collier and attempted to defend contemporary drama. But it is apparent from the number of editions sold (seven almost immediately) that Collier had the better of this quarrel.[24] If Vanbrugh felt he was a better moralist than Collier, it was apparent that a large part of the theatergoing audience decided that they would take their morality from the pulpit rather than seek for it in stage comedy.[25] As for politics, Congreve, a Whig, suddenly found himself on the wrong side. William's popularity declined after the Treaty of Ryswick. His ministers were put on trial; his request for troops to fend off a new threat from France was turned down by Parliament; and the Tory Party began a gradual rise to power that only ended in 1714 with the death of Queen Anne.

Congreve gave up writing comedies in 1700, but his reputation and the reputation of his comedies remained relatively high to his death in 1729. Indeed Arthur Scouten considered the fact that Congreve continued to be performed as much as he was during the second quarter of the eighteenth century to be a "quite remarkable achievement."[26] The point is that despite the popularity of his plays, they had to confront the general moral disapproval of his plays as being the product of an "Archetypal Libertine." Davies's hope that Garrick might revise *The Old Batchelor* was rewarded in 1788–89. But the nineteenth century, even more moral in many ways than its predecessor, saw a decline of interest in his plays. And even those who appreciated the frivolity of his comedies were hardly prepared to search his writings for serious intellectual content.

3

This brings me to a consideration of Congreve's "novel," *Incognita*. My approach to Congreve's writings in this volume is through the ideas they convey, both broadly philosophical and political. As mentioned earlier, Congreve was seriously committed to the "Revolutionary Principles" voiced by the Whigs during the Glorious Revolution of 1688 and so much a part of the politics of the reigns of William and Mary and then of William III. And as his writings reveal, he appears to have been equally committed to the philosophical empiricism of the time—a view that acknowledged that we know the world only through our perception of it through our senses. As McKenzie demonstrates, Congreve was writing his plays long before Bishop Berkeley was advancing his ideas. Nevertheless, he suggests that Congreve must have adopted John Locke's concept of a world that, however much it possessed its own reality, was perceived only through the human senses. McKenzie argues that the influence of Locke or a somewhat similar epistemology is apparent in Congreve's *The Mourning Bride*. I agree with this judgment and will examine it more fully in my chapter on Congreve's play, but what I want to do in this section of my chapter is examine the way another Lockean concept—that of identity—was to play a role in Congreve's novella, *Incognita*. Locke pointed out that it was not ideas that cause confusion as to identity but rather the names that we give to ideas, "whose identity and diversity will always be perceived as soon and clearly as the ideas themselves are."[27] Congreve appeared to have been fascinated by the ways in which the confusion of names can cause a confusion of identity. Locke's *Essay Concerning Human Understanding* first appeared in 1690; Congreve's novel was licensed in 1691 and published early in 1692. What I am trying to do in this section of my introduction is not to show any kind of direct influence of Locke on Congreve but rather to suggest that they shared the same philosophic ambience.

I don't want to burden a relatively light work such as *Incognita* with overly heavy significance. Yet from the beginning of this study I do want to insist on Congreve as an artist who not only appreciated the philosophic aspects of Vanbrugh and the epistemology and politics of John Locke but later in life clearly attached himself to the more profound speculations of Bishop Berkeley. In dealing with Congreve's plays, I will sometimes insist on complex meanings underlying what may appear as a relatively formulaic comedy of the period. This same complexity is present in *Incognita*, for from almost the very start of

Congreve's "novel," everything depends upon the play between disguise and true identity.[28] But identity, according to Locke, was to consist not so much in the body as in the mind—in the memory of whom one was and continued to be.[29] Nevertheless, matters were complicated. For example, in Britain through much of the eighteenth century, masquerades were attacked as evil because they permitted a loss of identity. It was not apparent that the wearer of the mask took on the identity displayed, but it was felt with considerable certainty that the central self was somehow compromised, especially with women. At the end of Congreve's novella, *Incognita* (Juliana), the unknown is introduced by Aurelian to his father, Don Fabio, and we are told that she was "differing nothing from *Juliana* but in her Name."[30] With this, "Love and Duty" are reconciled. In thinking they were defying their parents, Aurelian and Juliana actually discover that they have obeyed their parents' wishes while satisfying their own desires.

There is much of Shakespeare's *Romeo and Juliet* in Congreve's charming novel, including Juliet's famous speech wishing that Romeo could "doff that name that is no part" of him. I will examine the resemblances and differences between Shakespeare's tragedy and Congreve's novel later in this chapter. But at this point I want to discuss Congreve's play on names and essence, on the exteriority of clothes and interior worth, on silence being potentially startling, and darkness arousing the sense of sight. All of these subjects appear to engage with concepts that Locke was to discuss in his *Essay Concerning Human Understanding*. The world that humans experience through their senses is far different from the "real" world. But love is presented as an experience that can transform the self, and in general, the world of human experience is filled with danger—with passion, with hatred, and with duels. For the most part, the characters live in a world of disguises, of masks, costumes, and language that need to be penetrated if anything resembling truth is to be ascertained.

Incognita (Juliana) herself, resisting her father's choice of a mate for her, seems to find falling in love with Aurelian, disguised as Hippolito, that much easier. Similarly, Aurelian thinks of Hippolito as a "second self" (3:8 [l. 47]). The barriers of identities do not seem at all as absolute as one might expect. In beginning his discussion of names, Locke remarked, "All things that exist being particulars, it may perhaps be thought that words, which ought to be conformed to things, should be so too,—I mean in their signification; but yet we find quite the contrary."[31] Locke then proceeds to treat with the formation of general names and attack the concept of real essences, concluding that essences amount to no more than the bundling of things together for easier communication. He then went on to discuss how certain senses are needed to understand the nature of things; a blind man not being able to understand what a color was like. But for the most part language may be used for communication, and when things or ideas were discovered by Adam, he gave them particular names.

Incognita is very much about the distinction between names and essences. The masking of everyone at the celebration attended by Aurelian and Hippolito in Florence leads to the general belief that all the women are beautiful; and the women regard the two young men as wonderfully handsome. But their costumes give themselves a problematic identity as Hippolito ends up with that belonging to a well-known gallant of the town. Aurelian opens a conversation with Incognita by speculating on the relationship between costume and character. Incognita is for the most part more witty than Aurelian, but she is as attracted to him as he to her. They do not know the name of the other party, but they are drawn together by sympathy. Meanwhile, Hippolito, because of his costume, finds he is mistaken for a Don Lorenzo, who is deeply involved in the dueling rife society of Florence. On the other hand, when Leonora, the lady who warns him, takes off her mask, Hippolito is instantly attracted. Meanwhile Aurelian, when asked for his name by Incognita, decides, by way of responding to Incognita's request, to provide her with the name Hippolito, thus dropping the literal mask he has been wearing while assuming a different disguise, and in so doing deciding to take the "Character" of Hippolito. She, on the other hand, continues to retain the name of Incognita. Then Aurelian, coming back to his lodgings in the dark, finds himself involved in a sword fight with the real Hippolito.

After a sighing contest, the result of their new loves, the two friends decide that Hippolito will take on the name of Aurelian in dealing with Leonora. This complicates matters for Leonora, but she finds herself at least half in love with him. This occurs partly because Hippolito fit the general character of a fine gentleman that she liked. At the joust, the ladies recognize their admirers by specific signs. The lovers come together at the end as their irate parents confront them. Don Mario discovers that his daughter, Leonora, has not married Aurelian, as he thought, but rather Hippolito. Don Fabio, irate at the love expressed for Incognita (Juliana), is delighted to discover that the woman chosen by his son is actually Juliana, the daughter of the Marquess of Viterbo, a marriage that the parents had previously agreed upon. In concluding that "their Loves and Duty were reconciled" (3:62 [ll. 2134–35]), Congreve's narrator brings together two abstract concepts, often in conflict in human experience and here made to harmonize.

If I have turned Congreve's narrative into an abstract conflict of names by diminishing the real passions felt by the characters, it is because that is what Congreve's novel is actually about. As mentioned earlier, it might seem that the use of names is no more complex than Juliet's wish that Romeo could rid himself that name that is "no part of" him. Indeed, as hinted at earlier, there may be a bit of Shakespeare's *Romeo and Juliet* in Congreve's work.[32] But in its play with experience, Congreve is more indebted to John Locke and some of his contemporaries than he is to William Shakespeare. At one point, the narrator toys with the notion of Aurelian being startled by silence, explaining to the reader that, in this case, the absence of sensory experience can be as vivid an experience as the sudden deprivation of sight, explaining how: "[...] a Parallel Instance of Light; which though it does chiefly entertain the Eyes, and is indeed the prime Object of the Sight, yet should it immediately cease, to have a man left in the Dark by a suddain deficiency of it, would make him stare with his Eyes, and though he could not see, endeavor to look about him" (3:45 [ll. 1494–1500]). Not many contemporary novels stop the flow of the narrative to set forward a theory of sensory perception.

The world of *Incognita* is one of a reality in which identity is disguised by names, bodies are disguised by clothes, and imagined feelings are sometimes betrayed, sometimes enhanced by actual experience. The somewhat cynical narrator questions the ways in which the young automatically reject what their elders intend for them. Emotional attachments are formed by a certain association of ideas, and the imagination plays an important role in every meeting of the lovers. Leonora sings a song overheard by Hippolito in which she speaks of an unhappy maid being betrayed into love almost entirely by her imagination and then, once having actually seen him, "*'tis Hell/ To have him but in Thought*" (3:55 [ll. 1884–85]). Hippolito marries Leonora still under the disguise of Aurelian and only reveals himself when they have made their way to the scene at the lodgings of the two friends that unravels all the deception, all the false identifications for the revelation of the real personalities. *Incognita* has a happy end because, for all the disguises assumed by the main characters, they are—from a psychological standpoint—precisely what they claim to be.

In his poem, "Of Pleasing," Congreve warned against affectation as the worst of sins:

None are, so being what they are, in fault
But for not being what they wou'd be thought. (2:407)

In this poem, the faults of human beings are not savaged as they are in the satires of Swift. Their foibles are treated with relative gentleness, but as with the father who cannot recall where he put aside the book on improving the memory that he planned to give to his son out of affection for him, such weaknesses open all of us to comic moments. The lovers in *Incognita* all consider themselves to be completely free agents, despite their youth and need for parental approval. They discover at the end that this was at least partly illusory.

In offering this view of Congreve as a serious thinker, I am preparing a way into his plays that allows for complex interpretations. None of this negates the immediacy of his comic sense. Yet even here, according to contemporary descriptions, the laughter of the audience was a somewhat delayed experience, with some responding long after others, producing a strange effect of continuous reactions from those present. My interpretations will be in the broadest sense political, that is, involving the politics of a time of revolutionary transformation, with supporters of William and Mary believing in a notion of the state based on Parliament's power to choose a monarch, being witness to what has been called the "Financial Revolution," and approving William's war against Louis XIV. It was a divided society, with supporters of William and Mary, such as Congreve, living alongside and often associating with those, such as the Jacobites, who felt a metaphysical attachment to the monarchy and the family of James II and saw nothing problematic in supporting a French invasion of their native country along with a monarch who would be dependent upon France's monarch, Louis XIV. For the Jacobites and many Tories, this was not a time of any permanence. For Whigs, such as Congreve, it was a time for the free exploration of this new society.

Notes

1. See Thomas D'Urfey, *The Intrigues of Versailles: A Jilt in All Humours* (London, 1697), sig. A2.
2. See *The Development of English Drama in the Late Seventeenth Century* (Oxford: Clarendon Press, 1976).
3. Locke's fullest discussion of identity did not appear until the second edition in 1694, and I am using that edition for that reason. The subject was given currency during the seventeenth century through the philosophy of René Descartes. In 1687, for example, Gottfried Leibniz wrote to a friend, "The intelligent soul, that knows what it is [...] not only remains the same metaphysically [...], but it also remains morally the same and constitutes the same personality. For it is the memory and knowledge of this me that makes it liable to punishment and reward." Quoted in Galen Strawson, *Locke on Personal Identity: Consciousness and Concernment* (Princeton, NJ: Princeton University Press, 2011), 89.
4. D. F. McKenzie, "Richard Van Bleeck's Painting of William Congreve as Contemplative (1715)," *Review of English Studies* 51 (2000): 41–61.
5. Bernard Mandeville, *The Fable of the Bees*, 2 vols., ed. F. B. Kaye (Oxford: Clarendon Press, 1957), 1:324.
6. John Vanbrugh, *The Relapse*, in *Works*, ed. Bonamy Dobrée, 2 vols. (London: Nonesuch, 1927), 1:54.
7. Ibid., 1:54.
8. Ibid., 1:93.
9. Ibid., 1:93.
10. John Vanbrugh, *The Provok'd Wife*, in *Complete Works*, ed. Bonamy Dobrée and Geoffrey Webb, 4 vols. (London: Nonesuch, 1927), 1:117.
11. Ibid., 1:123.
12. Ibid., 1:169.
13. Samuel Pufendorf, *Law of Nature* (London, 1703), 75–110.
14. Thomas Davies, *Life of Garrick*, 2 vols. (London, 1780), 2:324.
15. Maximillian Novak, "Congreve as the Eighteenth Century Archetypal Libertine," *Restoration and Eighteenth Century Theatre Research* 15 (1976): 35–39.

16 *William Congreve: The Critical Heritage*, ed. Alexander Lindsay and Howard Erskine-Hill (London: Routledge, 1989), 188–89.
17 See Edmond Burke, *Congreve: the Critical Heritage*, ed. Alexander Lindsay and Howard Erskine Hill (London: Routledge, 1989), 219–20.
18 Samuel Johnson, *Lives of the English Poets*, introd. Arthur Waugh, 2 vols. (London: Oxford University Press, 1972), 2:27.
19 Ibid., 2:28.
20 Many critics replying to Collier saw similarities between Collier and Prynne. See for example, Anon., *The Stage Acquitted* (London, 1699), 11; and Edward Filmer, *A Defence of Plays: Or the Stage Vindicated, from several Passages in Mr. Collier's Short View* (London, 1707), 42.
21 Johnson, *Lives of the Poets*, 27.
22 Matthew Kinservik, *Disciplining Satire: The Censorship of Satiric Comedy on the Eighteenth-Century London Stage* (Lewisburg: Bucknell University Press, 2002), 39–49.
23 Among a variety of misapprehensions from Johnson was the notion that Collier would have been pleased to see the gradual reformation of the theater during his later years. The not so hidden agenda of Collier was the complete abolition of theatrical performances. See Johnson, *Lives of the Poets*, 2:28.
24 See Yuji Kaneko, ed. *A Short View of the Immorality and Profaneness of the English Stage*, by Jeremy Collier (London: Routledge, 1996), v.
25 For a discussion of the stage as providing genuine moral instruction and the argument against such a view, see George Ridpath, *The Stage Acquitted: Being a Full Answer to Mr. Collier, and the Other Enemies of the Drama* (London, 1699), 79, 80, 129. George Ridpath, a defender of Collier, made the seriousness of contemporary comedy an important argument for its abolition.
26 *The London Stage*, ed. Arthur Scouten et al., 11 vols. (Carbondale: Southern Illinois University Press, 1960–1968), Part 3, 1729–47 [vol. 6], cxlix.
27 John Locke, *An Essay Concerning Human Understanding*, ed. Alexander Fraser, 2 vols. (Oxford: Oxford University Press, 1891; reprint Dover Press, 1959), 2:170.
28 In her essay, on *Incognita*, Aspasia Velissariou is mainly concerned with problems of rank, but she does allow for some "epistemological play" with matters of identity. See "The Vicissitudes of Resemblance in Congreve's *Incognita*," *Journal of the Short Story* 39 (2002): 23–40.
29 For those concentrating on memory in Locke's *Essay*, such as Antony Flew, the most essential section is II, xxvii, 1–29. Others, such as Philippe Hamou, while admitting the importance of memory in Locke's concept of identity, point to the concept of a *train of Ideas* (II, xiv, 3) that provides a sense of succession and duration and therefore "the continuation of the existence of ourselves." See Antony Flew, "Locke and the Problem of personal Identity," in *Locke and Berkeley*, ed. C. B. Martin and D. M. Armstrong (New York: Anchor Books, 1968), 155–58; and Philippe Hamou, "On Selves and Thinking Substances," in *Locke and Cartesian Philosophy*, ed. Philippe Hamou and Martine Pécharmon (Oxford: Oxford University Press, 2018), 120–43.
30 William Congreve, *The Works of William Congreve*, ed. D. F. McKenzie and C. Y. Ferdinand, 3 vols. (Oxford: Oxford University Press, 2011), 3:61. Subsequent quotations from *Incognita* will refer to this text.
31 Locke, *Essay*, 2:14 (Book 3, chapter 3, section 1).
32 Congreve clearly drew upon Shakespeare's tragedy when he came to write *The Mourning Bride*. See p. 8 and the comments of the editors in the second volume of Congreve's *Works*, 567–68.

Chapter 3

THE "FASHIONABLE CUTT OF THE TOWN" AND WILLIAM CONGREVE'S *THE OLD BATCHELOR*

The Romantic critics, led by Charles Lamb, advanced the argument that the scenes portrayed in Restoration drama belonged to a kind of imaginary world having no relationship to reality. They did so by way of searching for a method of defending these plays against the charges of obscenity and immorality leveled against them by a variety of moralists who followed Jeremy Collier's examination and condemnation of these works in 1698.[1] As Jonas Barish has demonstrated, "anti-theatrical prejudice" has always accompanied stage productions; even J.-J. Rousseau had weighed in against stage performances in the middle of the eighteenth century.[2] If many thought of the theater as objectionable in principle, how much more unacceptable were plays that dealt openly with sexuality and the details of contemporary life? The Romantic approach prevailed for a time, but it eventually brought with it the possibility of dismissing these plays on the grounds that they had no relevance to ordinary life. Such an attitude dominated the middle of the twentieth century and it has only been during the last thirty-five years that these plays have been regarded as seriously reflecting the Restoration experience. More particularly, critics have become aware of how thoroughly politics pervaded the drama of the time and how entirely the playwrights devoted themselves to political statements and attacks upon the attitudes of their opponents.[3]

By now, almost all of William Congreve's plays have been subjected to political readings. Many years ago I suggested that his sole tragedy, *The Mourning Bride*, might be read in terms of a Whig allegory in which the old forces of repression are swept away by the triumph of the young lovers, and somewhat later, I argued that *The Double Dealer* was essentially about the survival of the English family over the conspiracies of "Jack" (Jacobite) Maskwell.[4] Even more recently, Richard Braverman has maintained that *The Way of the World* embodies another Whiggish triumph—this time over another conspirator, Fainall, and his attempt to take over the wealth of Lady Wishfort.[5] Much the same might be said for *Love for Love*, with the victory of the true lovers,

Valentine and Angelica, over the Hobbist ideas of the tyrannical patriarch, Sir Sampson Legend. The play that involves the greatest problem for political interpretation, however, is *The Old Batchelor*, for most contemporaries appeared to think that for Congreve's stage debut, he had written a play that avoided the type of backbiting, lampooning, and political innuendoes that distinguished the comedies of the early 1690s.

Such a judgment, however, must be viewed in the context of the times. Satire had emerged as the form, which, to paraphrase Juvenal, writers could not avoid if they wanted to do so. Dryden had given satire a new prominence with his translations of Juvenal and Persius accompanied by his "Preface to the Satires," in which he had written some of his most acute criticism. For Jacobites such as Dryden and his sometime collaborator, Thomas Southerne, half concealing satiric barbs under seemingly innocent historical parallels became an art in itself. As Philip Harth has pointed out, the enterprise was very different in nature from his direct party propaganda during the 1680s, but through allusion, parallels, and innuendoes, Dryden continued to wage poetic warfare against the government of William and Mary and William III throughout the entire decade of the 1690s.[6] The audience for Dryden's poems, translations, and plays, and indeed the audience for every work of the time, came to the literary experience prepared to discover every possible innuendo, social as well as political. This was particularly true of theatrical presentations. For example, during the 1690s, the playwright Thomas D'Urfey frequently added disclaimers to his printed plays, insisting that he was not lampooning individuals who thought they had been attacked in his comedies.[7] On at least one occasion, when Queen Mary went to the theater, the audience apparently turned to her to see how she reacted to lines that could be interpreted as reflecting upon her relationship to her deposed father, James II.[8] The response of the audience was symptomatic of the expectation for political innuendo at the time.[9]

It is not surprising that the word "innuendo" was given its modern meanings at around this time. Formerly, it had a meaning equivalent to "in other words" by way of explaining a difficult or ambiguous concept. During the political squabbles at the end of Charles II's reign, two related meanings emerged. An innuendo might be, as it is usually today, an "oblique hint, indirect suggestion [...] esp. of a depreciating kind," or it might be "an interpolated or appended explanation of, or construction put upon a word, expression or passage; esp. the injurious meaning or signification alleged to be conveyed by words not *per se* injurious or actionable" (*OED*). Although the *OED* gives the usage of Roger L'Estrange in 1678 as its point of origin, its popular usage as a kind of hint or implied meaning dates from the trials associated with the Rye House Plot and the persecutions of those considered enemies of the crown in and after

1683. The most famous use of "innuendo" as extrapolated meaning came in the trial of Algernon Sidney, who was convicted on the basis of an interpretation of a reading in a manuscript found on his desk. Chief Justice Jeffreys maintained that a general argument about the rights of the people to remove tyrants might be constructed as a direct attack on Charles II.[10] Thereafter, contemporary writers on politics spoke of his being convicted on the basis of an "innuendo."[11]

In some ways, however, an even more elaborate use of "innuendo" came in the trial of the dissenting minister, Thomas Rosewell, around the same time (1684). As in the case of Sidney, the presiding judge was the infamous Jeffreys. Jeffreys used the concept of innuendo in its original meaning as well as in both of its contemporary meanings. He accused Rosewell of hinting at Charles II's sexual life in his references to Samson and Delilah and of "imagining" the death of Charles in allusions to the deaths of wicked kings, even though Rosewell stated that Ahab and his son Ahaziah were intended.[12] The prosecution argued that Rosewell's case was similar to the trial of Algernon Sidney and that the jury should come in with another guilty verdict. Rosewell's side argued that words should not be drawn out of their proper signification, that in matters of law, one should not "press Words, or strain them to speak more than willingly they mean or intend."[13] At one point, both Jeffreys and the defense became so entangled in the problems of determining the exact meaning of an innuendo that Rosewell's lawyer expressed his wish that all discussions of innuendoes might be dropped from the trial. Although Rosewell was found guilty, he was pardoned by Charles II and his sentence reduced to a fine, after Sir John Talbot had appealed to the king and convinced him that if the principles applied in the Rosewell case were allowed to stand, no Englishman would feel safe from prosecution.[14] Why Talbot felt this way is easy enough to ascertain. At one point during the trial, Jeffreys had speculated that the audience, which had listened to Rosewell's sermon, might be presumed to have been infected by his alleged innuendoes and therefore be as guilty of treason as the unfortunate preacher. Algernon Sidney became a Whig martyr and Thomas Rosewell a hero to the Dissenters, but their cases, in addition to popularizing new meanings to an old word, may have given some impetus to a literary culture in which the audience, already attuned to discovering hidden meanings and political references, was even more eager to search for concealed allusions.

As has been suggested, after the Glorious Revolution, it was the Jacobites who became most skillful at the game of hidden meanings, but if satire was the most obvious vehicle for attacking William and Mary, it was also the most dangerous. As an alternative, playwrights opposed to the regime often turned to historical plays that might offer political parallels to contemporary events.

If audiences might make the application, it was surely not the fault of the author, or so, at least, Dryden would argue in his defense.[15] And if the playgoer wished to construe a contemporary political parallel from an old play such as *The Spanish Fryar*, how much more might they look for it in contemporary performances?

In Dryden's case, the question is: Could he ever resist the temptation to hint at a subversive political meaning? Some time ago, in watching a delightful—if abridged—performance of Dryden's *King Arthur* by *Les Arts Florissants*, I found myself very much in the position of what must have been that of the audience that heard it in 1691.[16] I had not read the play for several years and had never seen it performed. Of course the music of Purcell was wonderful, but what of the politics? Shortened as it was, the text still seemed to bristle with possible political significance. Was this simply a story of a legendary Arthur who restores Britain to its true greatness, or was it all about the deposed James II, and his true claim to the nation? Were the "Saxon" hordes really William's Dutch soldiers? And was it an accident that both the evil enchanter and the leader of the enemy forces had names beginning with O—like William of Orange? Doubtless most members of the audience were content to listen to the wonderful music and watch the spectacle, but surely Dryden hoped the audience could take away some kind of political message. Later in this chapter I will discuss some of Dryden's use of the drama for more overt attacks upon the government, but I choose to start with *King Arthur* because it might be read as entirely free of political propaganda.

Although he admits that *King Arthur* was "open to a Jacobite reading," James Winn argues that the opera was so balanced in its possible political ramifications that supporters of William could read it in a positive way and the Jacobites might read it as an anti-Williamite play.[17] Everything suggests that Winn read Dryden's intentions correctly, but who in the audience did not know of Dryden's political position? In his dedication to Halifax, Dryden himself speaks of how he felt obliged to alter the politics of the work from his original draft that had been written in 1684, but his claim to have had the full approbation of Queen Mary for his work has been greeted with considerable skepticism.[18] And while modern readers might find his references to the strength of the navy protecting England's shores to be a simple statement of patriotism, what contemporary reader did not know of the defeat inflicted by the French upon the combined British-Dutch fleet at Beachy Head on June 30, 1690? Not until after the end of the naval battle at La Hogue on May 20, 1692, was it evident that James II was not going to be capable of launching an invasion of Britain. In his notes to the play, Vinton Dearing suggests the possibility of irony in several places, but the various parts of the published text, including the prologue, epilogue, and its dedication, read more like a work written in coded language, with the knowledgeable audience having no difficulty supplying the true meaning of what might seem innocuous enough to many readers.[19]

It was not merely in the theater and in satires that the Jacobite message was conveyed. The author of *Antiquity Reviv'd: Or, the Government of a Certain Island Anciently Call'd Astreada* (1693) put his criticism of the new world of William and Mary into a prose utopia.[20] Any punishment that might have followed the publication of this work was deflected by the notation that the society being described dated "Some hundreds of yrs before Christ." It begins innocuously enough with the story of how some Athenians fled their city by sea after the conquest by Alexander. Blown to an unknown island, the Athenian exiles encounter the world of the Astreadans and are immediately enchanted by their ideas on religion and philosophy. Only after more than fifty pages might the reader become aware that he/she was not reading the kind of imaginary voyage that, in the hands of Gabriel Foigny and Denis Vairasse, insinuated certain deistical and radical political notions at the end of the seventeenth century. After a discussion of the religion of the Astreadans, which consists of a general worship of "Providence," without any belief in miracles, the text veers suddenly to a discussion of politics clearly representative of the Jacobite viewpoint. There is no *original Contract* between the monarch and the people. The system is entirely patriarchal, with the monarch having absolute power. The notion that the people would have the right to make laws is viewed as absurd, and the monarch, who represents virtue in the nation, has the power to crush any kind of popular threat to his family or the state. Of course there were direct attacks upon the government along with advocacy for the return of James II such as *Great Britain's Just Complaint for Her Late Measures, Present Sufferings, and Future Miseries She Is Exposed To* (1691?), but most of the writers who opposed the reign of William and Mary appeared to believe that indirect methods were best. Religion, warfare, the rise of the monied interests, and foreign domination were all subjects that could be hinted at in utopias, vaguely parallel dramatic plots or verse satires containing obscure references.

2

In his prologue to *The Old Batchelor*, Congreve describes the new satiric mode, which might be found in its quintessential state in the prologues to these recent plays and tries to distinguish his play from these bitterly satiric comedies:

> But now, no more like Suppliants, we come:
> A Play makes War, and Prologue is the Drum:
> Arm'd with keen Satyr, and with pointed Wit,

> We threaten you who do for Judges sit,
> To save our Plays, or else we'll damn your Pit.
> But for your Comfort, it falls out to day,
> We've a young Author and his first born Play;
> So, standing only on his good Behaviour,
> He's very civil, and entreats your Favour.[21]

Congreve was successful in this attempt at presenting his play as an example of "Humour" without any elements of satire or serious themes,[22] yet for all its apparent apolitical surface and its charming allusiveness to earlier comedies, *The Old Batchelor* contains much topical satire along with an unusually ambiguous ending for Vainlove and Araminta, who share the main love interest of the play with Bellmour and Belinda. Like many texts, both those favorable to the reign of William and Mary and the political principles of the Glorious Revolution and those favorable to the Jacobite cause, this play has a feeling about it of cynicism, open-endedness, and, particularly in the Heartwell plot, bitterness. Its enormous success, though dependent in part on the expectation aroused over a play that had been long in preparation as well as upon the play's intrinsic excellence, had to be linked to its ability to capture the mood of the times.

Congreve's biographer, William Hodges, was convinced that Congreve wrote the play in 1689, based on the assertion in his dedication that the original version had been written four years earlier.[23] Congreve later remarked that he had composed it during a "slow Recovery from a Fit of Sickness," and the place of composition was likely to have been outside of London in either Ilam, Derbyshire, or in the nearby Stretton Hall, Staffordshire.[24] D. Crane Taylor suggested that William accompanied his father and mother to England after the death of his grandfather in August 1688, but Hodges also speculated that, like so many others, the Congreve family fled Dublin for political reasons.[25] The earl of Tyrconnel had been rooting out Protestants from the army as early as 1686, and in 1689, Congreve's father was listed as an unemployed army officer in the London environs. Tyrconnel's vendetta extended itself to Trinity College, the Protestant university, where Congreve was studying. With both students and tutors fleeing precipitously during the months preceding William of Orange's landing at Taunton on November 5, 1688, it must have seemed as if Ireland would be an uncomfortable place for those who did not support James II. Under these circumstances, Congreve would have seemed an unlikely writer to have demonstrated unhappiness with James II's departure from England or to have written a comedy that would have been skeptical about William III's war against Louis XIV, James's chief defender on the continent.

At any rate, Congreve appears to have written the first draft of his play in a place that he described as "so much out of the world that nothing but [...] great news could have reacht it."[26] That he would have known every detail about all the "Murmurers," who were to be so critical of the Glorious Revolution and publish their discontent in satires and lampoons, seems improbable.[27] Yet Congreve's play is very much the product of 1691 and 1692, when anticlerical satire was all the rage and when Jacobites saw the country as still "unsettled" and ready for a new restoration of the Stuarts. Even if Congreve was not following the news closely, his situation and that of his family would have meant that the outlines of the political situation would have been clear and inescapable to him.

Thomas Southerne, a constant supporter of the House of Stuart both before and after James II fled England, described how he helped Congreve "in the whole course of his play,"[28] which may mean that he acted as a kind of contact with the managers of the theater or that he added something to the writing. Southerne also turned it over to John Dryden, the disgruntled former laureate, for revision. Dryden, Southerne tells us, thought it an admirable "first play," but judged that "the Author not being acquainted with the Stage or the town, it woud be pity to have it miscarry for want of a little Assistance: the stuff was rich indeed, it wanted only the fashionable cutt of the town" (151). Southerne continued, "To help that Mr Dryden, Mr Arthur Manwyring, and Mr Southerne red it with great care, and Mr Dryden put it in the order it was playd" (151).

The passage is puzzling. Mainwaring was to become one of the most effective of Whig polemicists during the party wars of Queen Anne's reign, but at this time, he, like Dryden and Southerne, was a Jacobite. Although the notion that Dryden rearranged the play has been greeted with skepticism, it is possible that he reshaped the play in many ways.[29] After all, how could Congreve, at the time a young and completely inexperienced playwright, resist the help of the best poet and one of the best dramatists of the Restoration? The deposed laureate had returned to writing for the stage with *Don Sebastian* (1689) and *Amphytrion* (1690), both of which had considerable success.

On the other hand, both of Dryden's plays have strong Jacobite subtexts. If, as has been suggested, *King Arthur* appeared to deliver an anti-Williamite message by innuendoes and coded language, the intent of a number of Dryden's other plays is apparent enough. His *Cleomenes* (1691) was originally barred from the stage by the government for just such a reason. Under such conditions, we may well wonder whether, when Dryden remarked that the play "wanted only the fashionable cutt of the town," he might not have meant that it needed a strong dose of the kind of innuendo and satire that the Jacobites and enemies of William were spreading throughout the nation—satire upon the clergy, most of whom had turned their backs upon James II to take oaths of loyalty to King William, and upon the war against Louis XIV, which the Jacobites argued to be unwinnable, costly from the standpoint of English lives lost, and generally futile.

Amphytrion: Or the Two Sosias (1690) was typical of such propaganda.[30] The story of how Zeus took the place of Amphytrion, the legitimate husband of Alcmena, had intercourse with her, and through this action eventually produced Hercules may be open to any number of interpretations, but in Dryden's hands, the play becomes a vehicle for raising questions about William III's claim to the throne and about England's role in the process. The wife's willingness to accept a surrogate lover—a being of great power—in place of her authentic husband provides a jarring note to the low comedy of the servants. Though Hercules was traditionally to become a benefactor to mankind, his role is also put in doubt by Dryden's rendering of the theme. Since William III was frequently associated with Hercules in the propaganda written in his praise, few of the knowledgeable members of the audience would have missed the allusion.[31] In addition, Dryden's attack upon the very notion of the hero resonated with specific acerbity throughout the play. Dryden, like Hamlet, could claim that the story was well known and that he was innocent of any kind of malice, but the play was nevertheless a trap for the ruling king. As has been mentioned, audiences of the 1690s went to the theater expecting just such a thrill afforded by parallel stories of this kind.[32] But if Dryden's *King Arthur* depended on coded references and innuendo, his *Amphytrion* was closer to true irony.

Paradoxically, *The Old Batchelor* was both the most contemporary of Congreve's plays from the standpoint of its allusions to current topics and the most formulaic, in many ways a pastiche of the dozens of previous comedies written after the Restoration of Charles II. This seeming contradiction may be compared to the dilemma in Jorge Luis Borges's "Pierre Menard, Author of the *Quixote*." Borges suggests that if *Don Quixote* might be approached as a modern text, the language and meaning of Cervantes's masterpiece would be transformed and our understanding of it entirely changed.[33] Similarly, in the context of the 1690s, the comic situations and wit of the 1670s and 1680s assumed entirely new meanings in Congreve's reshaping of the older material. That at the very beginning Congreve's Vainlove should argue that his pursuit of pleasure was a form of business might sound like a fairly traditional opening for a Restoration comedy, a variation on the opening of Thomas Shadwell's *The Virtuoso* (1676). But in his defense of fashion and luxury as promoting the economic growth and well-being of society, Vainlove appears to be echoing a contemporary debate. Nicholas Barbon had recently argued the radical notion that the pursuits of pleasure, new fashions, and luxury were vital to the economic health of the country.³⁴ Although Bernard Mandeville was later to publicize and elaborate upon this paradox in the various versions of the *Fable of the Bees* (1705, 1714, 1723, etc.), Barbon, with his stress upon encouraging consumption, had already given currency to this idea. The opening of the play, then, with its ironic emphasis on ways of enriching the nation through the pursuit of luxury and pleasure, placed it squarely in the world of the 1690s, that time of the financial revolution, lotteries, and projects.

On the other hand, the criticism of Fondlewife, the banker, and his pursuit of money belongs to the counterattack upon the new commercialism and the rise to importance of those dealing in finance.³⁵ Ned Ward's *The Miracles Perform'd by Money* (1692) viewed the entire society as corrupted by the emphasis upon wealth. Money, he argued, will transform workers into gentlemen; mothers will betray their daughters for money; and the displacement of a respect for authority, by money, will eventually turn the manners and morals of the society upside down. Ward specifically complains about situations such as that which occurs between Fondlewife and Laetitia, in which an old, impotent husband, who is rich, may purchase a young wife.

> Women like *Books* and Pictures now a Days,
> Are put to Sale, and who the Price can Raise,
> Not he whose merits decently can Crave'em,
> No, no, the lucky He bids most shall have 'em:
> Youth, Wit and Valour will not prevail:
> But Yet *Almighty Money* cannot fail.³⁶

A similar lament by Robert Gould, in his poem *The Corruption of the Times by Money* (1693), placed the character of men such as Fondlewife among the destroyers of the country.³⁷ William III's Holland may have been content to think of itself as a commercial country, but England had some time to go before it would be entirely content with such a designation.

Even Fondlewife's designation as a "banker" is significant because it functions in an entirely new context. The play was performed one year before the establishment of the Bank of England, but discussions concerning various forms of banks were everywhere.³⁸ While the bank was instrumental in enabling William to finance the War of the Grand Alliance, the Tories and Jacobites were to regard it with suspicion and hostility. Although the departure of the husband to his scene of business and the abandonment of the young wife recalls Wycherley's *The Country Wife* (1676), the general anti-commercial context of such an action was now much richer. Fondlewife's business is obscure, but it does have to do with a shipping investment at a time when the complaints about the losses at sea, through the depredations of the French fleet and privateers, fueled the criticism of the Murmerers and Grumbletonians.[39] There were some specific scandals that appear to have informed Congreve's text as well. In *The Trimming Court Divine* of 1690, the Jacobite author drew an analogy between the political situation and a recent event involving the young wife of an old lawyer who had been carried off by a galant.[40] In fact, the author of *The Trimming Court Divine* touched on most of the problems of the time. Some of these involved England's war on the continent, which the Jacobites argued to be endless, incapable of ending in victory for the English, and a drain of English money and lives.

The characters of the cowardly Captain Bluffe, who claims to have fought in Flanders, the timid Sir Joseph Wittol, who longs to be associated with a heroic soldier, and Sharper, who cheats Sir Joseph out of his money, have to be read within these contexts. That figures such as Sharper, who is little better than a con man, appeared everywhere in the plays of these years, whether by Whig or Tory playwrights, is hardly surprising since everyone viewed this as a time of dubious schemes and projects. The government itself was constantly promoting schemes to raise money for the war, including unusual forms of taxation and lotteries. Sharper's proverbial, "'Tis an ill wind that blows nobody good" (1:32 [II.i, 30–31]), aside from expressing the prevailing views of self-interest and opportunism, might well have been heard by the audience as a reference to those who flourished after the famous "Providential" wind that blew William to England.[41]

Echoes of the ongoing war emerge everywhere in the text of Congreve's play, and there is no heroic soldier in the play to counter the cowardice of Sir Joseph Wittoll and his protector Bluffe. The audience had to perceive the ambiguity in Bluffe's boast that he fought only for "justifiable" causes such as his "country" or "religion" (Volume 1: 36 [II.ii, 21–22]). Was the war on the continent, sometimes called the War of the Grand Alliance, sometimes the Nine Years War, and in America referred to as King William's War, justifiable from an English standpoint? Certainly the Jacobites implied that it was not, but even strong supporters of the Glorious Revolution had their doubts. Many felt that England should limit itself to a naval war.[42] Such an attitude became even more popular after the stunning victory of the Dutch and English fleet at Cape La Hogue on May 19, 1692, which made the planned invasion of England by James II no longer a real possibility.

The ground war in Flanders seemed to many to be too distant a matter to involve the expenditure of English blood and English money. After the violent standoff at Steenkirk on July 24, 1692, which resulted in 8,000 casualties, it was rumored that the Dutch commander, Graf van Solms-Braunfels, was responsible for "allowing the British to die on the Plaine St. Martin out of hatred and callousness."[43] Rumors of this kind were spread by leaders of the

English troops such as Thomas Talmash and John Churchill in an effort to wrest power over the allied army from the Dutch, but they had some basis in fact. Following the battle of Steenkirk, British wounded were indeed left lying in the streets of Brussels while the Dutch troops were cared for in the Grootlegerhospitael. The British troops had fought bravely in a losing cause, as they were to do at Landen in 1693, and there was great pride in England at the courage they had shown.[44] Although the Jacobites and Tories were successfully arguing that Steenkirk had been a defeat that brought into question William's abilities as a leader, his supporters attempted to show that Steenkirk was actually close to being a victory, that the French suffered greater casualties, and that the British troops "have shewn by the Blood they have so chearfully spilt, what Affection and Fidelty they have to his [William's] Service."[45]

As a dramatic type, Bluffe much resembles the Pistol of Shakespeare's *Henry V*, but whatever his pedigree, he is used for some distinctly anti-Williamite satire on the indecisive and bloody Flanders campaign of 1691–92 during which, in addition to the indecisive battle of Steenkirk mentioned above, the allies lost the fortress of Namur. Sir Joseph Wittol may be seen as any Englishman so cowardly as to need a soldier who had fought in Flanders to protect him, and Bluffe's anger against the *London Gazette* for failing to mention his name in its accounts of battles, aside from the likelihood that he was never near a battlefield, seems to suggest the notion that soldiers are dominated by a desire for fame and that the reputation of someone such as William III might be more a matter of publicity than reality.[46] Bluffe's final speech, "No more Wars, Spouse, no more Wars" (1:121 [V.xv, 43]), may be taken as an inoffensive, comic resolution on his part to avoid becoming a cuckold, but it does have larger connotations about war and its evil influence upon private life. Such satire might be the "fashionable cutt of the Town," but it was hardly what might have been expected from the son of an army officer and the future poet who was to celebrate William's later victory at Namur in 1695 with a grandiose ode.

The attack upon the war is linked to the wickedness of the clergy in Bellmour's remark upon Bluffe as a fraud and a "pretender," who "wears the habit of a Soldier, which now a days as often cloaks Cowardice, as a Black Gown does Atheism" (1:29 [I.v, 27–29]). Although there was much fault found with the behavior of the clergy toward James II after many had gone back on their expressions of complete obedience, most criticisms of the clergy during the 1690s alluded to the crisis in the Church of England created by William Sherlock's decision to take the oaths of loyalty to William and Mary.[47] Sherlock had originally refrained from taking the oaths.[48] He had let the deadline pass before expressing his loyalty to the reigning monarchs, and many felt that his actions demonstrated that the leaders of the Church of England were acting entirely on the basis of self-interest rather than conviction.[49] Although Sherlock was to explain his decision on theological grounds—that the clergy had the duty to obey the established monarch—many of the satirists blamed Sherlock's decision on his wife, who was supposed to have insisted upon it.[50] Her motivation had nothing to do with theology. In Thomas D'Urfey's *The Weesils* (1691), she is depicted as objecting to the loss of income ("Cheese") that might result from her husband's initially principled stance.[51] The decision seemed to throw doubt upon all religious principles. The author of *The Moralists* (1691) put the matter succinctly. After having a pastor attack the morals of the age, the author remarks that the clergy had lost the credibility necessary for commenting convincingly upon ethical matters:

> And yet 'tis thought by more than half the Nation,
> That you have lately lost some Reputation.[52]

Visions of a world of cheat and deceit were ubiquitous in contemporary literature. Of course, the satire in Congreve's play seems mostly aimed at the Dissenters, but Jeremy Collier was right when he argued that Congreve had managed to "hook the *Church* of *England* into the Abuse."[53]

In Congreve's play, on the suggestion of Laetitia, Vainlove (for whom Bellmour acts as a substitute when Vainlove expresses a lack of interest) is supposed to come to her dressed as Parson Spintext while Fondlewife, her husband, is away. The very name suggests misusing holy texts, and like his disciple Fondlewife, Spintext appears to be married to a woman of easy virtue. His wife's name, Comfort, and his name, Tribulation, suggest much about their relationship. Bellmour's use of the cloak of religion to gain his ends with Laetitia also might be seen to have general implications at a time when, as one writer argued, the clergy of the Church of England appeared to be practicing "Sanctity in Masquerade," hiding their self-interest behind their clerical gowns.[54] Indeed, as Bellmour admits, had he carried *The Practice of Piety* with him instead of the novels of Scarron, he would never have been detected by Fondlewife. Similarly, the "blessings of an easy faith" (1:99 [IV. xxii, 139]) that allows Fondlewife to believe in Laetitia's innocence might seem to apply more generally to the faith of a Sherlock, who could discover reasons for taking the oath of loyalty to the reigning monarch. The "act of oblivion" (1:120 [V.xv, 5–6]), which pardons Captain Bluffe and Sir Joseph at the end, clearly alludes to the pardons extended to those who took the oaths belatedly. If Jeremy Collier was to perceive much in the play that he thought anticlerical and blasphemous, he was certainly right to the extent that Congreve's comedy added to undermining the credibility of both the nonjurors and those who had taken the oaths. In this, *The Old Batchelor* was, as has been mentioned, much in the same vein as Durfey's *The Moralists* with its attack upon "Sanctity in Masquerade."

What I am suggesting, then, is that by the time Congreve's Jacobite friends had finished with *The Old Batchelor*, it had some distinct features that are little in keeping with Congreve's other writings. I do not find even a hint of politics in his first publication, the novella *Incognita*, unless one would want to politicize the innocuous theme of reconciliation, but in *The Old Batchelor* satirical implication manages even to invade the traditional love plot with Bellinda using the imagery of creditors and debtors in speaking of Bellmour's love, and Araminta remarking, "Every Man now changes his Mistress and his Religion, as his Humour varies or his Interest" (1:46 [II.viii, 32–34]). Even Araminta's refusal to take Vainlove up on his proposal for fear that her very act of consenting would cause him to repent, suggests mental hesitations and an unsettled condition that may be seen to have larger implications for the state of England as a whole.

Would Congreve have permitted such rewritings? He may have been aware that he had fallen into a nest of Jacobites, but to repeat, this was, after all, his first play. What beginning playwright in England would have rejected suggestions from the nation's greatest poet? Besides, Congreve was famous for being inoffensive and able to get along with people of all political convictions.[55] Doubtless most of Congreve's "rich" dialogue that so impressed Dryden, Southerne, and Maynwaring remained, and the sensibility of Araminta was very much part of Congreve's gift to the comedies of the 1690s. But who can doubt that, given his convictions, Dryden would have wanted to provide the play with a little of the political thrust to be found in his reworking of Plautus's innocuous comedy into his ironic *Ampyhtrion: Or The Two Sosias*.

Notes

1 Charles Lamb, "On the Artificial Comedy of the Last Century," in *The Works of Charles and Mary Lamb*, ed E. V. Lucas (London: Methuen, 1912), 161–68.
2 Jonas Barish, *The Antitheatrical Prejudice* (Berkeley: University of California Press, 1981), especially 256–94.
3 See, e.g., Susan Owen's excellent discussion of the theater during the years of the Exclusion Crisis, *Restoration Theatre and Crisis* (Oxford: Clarendon Press, 1996).
4 Maximillian E. Novak, *Congreve* (New York: Twayne, 1970), 122–37; and "The Discourses of Criticism and the Discourses of History in the Restoration and Early Eighteenth Century," in *Theory and Tradition in Eighteenth-Century Studies*, ed Richard B. Schwartz (Carbondale: Southern Illinois University Press, 1990), 104–11.
5 Richard Braverman, *Plots and Counterplots* (Cambridge: Cambridge University Press, 1993), 213–37.

6 Philip Harth, *Pen for a Party: Dryden's Tory Propaganda in Its Contexts* (Princeton, NJ: Princeton University Press, 1993), 271. Of course, there was a major difference between writing satire with the full support of the government and writing as an opponent of the regime. Dryden could hardly have written a satire such as *The Medal* during the 1690s.

7 See, e.g., the preface to D'Urfey's *Love for Money: Or, the Boarding School* (London, 1691), sig A3v. For a complaint against contemporary satirists, especially D'Urfey, see *Wit for Money: Or Poet Stutter* (London, 1691), 11.

8 *The London Stage 1660–1800: A Calendar of Plays, Entertainments & Afterpieces Together with Casts, Box-Receipts and Contemporary Comment*, ed William Van Lennep et al. (Carbondale: Southern Illinois University Press, 1960–68), 1:371. The play was John Dryden's *The Spanish Friar*. The audience turned to observe Queen Mary's reaction "whenever their fancy led them to make any application."

9 For a discussion of the use of coded language and parallelism, see Richard Ashcraft and Alan Roper, *Politics as Reflected in Literature*, introduction by Maximillian E. Novak (Los Angeles, CA: William Andrews Clark Memorial Library, 1989).

10 See H. B. Irving, *The Life of Judge Jeffreys* (London: William Heinemann, 1898), 176.

11 The *OED* gives Bishop Gilbert Burnet's statement from 1715 on this subject (*History of His Own Time*, 4 vols. [London: Samuel Bagster, 1815], 2:220), but Burnet was simply repeating the use of innuendo at the time the event occurred.

12 See George Jeffries, *The Arraignment and Tryal of the Late Reverend Mr. Thomas Rosewell, for High-Treason; before the LordChief Jefferies* (London: 1715), 242, 247.

13 Ibid., 271.

14 Despite Jeffreys's well-earned reputation for ferocity toward defendants, he was genuinely concerned about the legal ramifications of convicting Rosewell on innuendoes, and at one point, when the government's solicitor blandly stated that a particular innuendo was clear, Jeffreys appeared to reject the entire notion of conviction on the basis of innuendo. "You have *Innuendo'd* it too much I do doubt," remarked Jeffreys, "for all the Facts are laid under an *Innuendo*, without a positive Averment." On the basis of being unable to determine whether an innuendo was intended, Jeffries allowed Rosewell to obtain counsel to argue the point. Jeffries, *Arraignment and Tryal of Thomas Rosewell*, 250.

15 See his dedication to *Cleomenes*.

16 The original performance was sometime in May 1691. The performance I witnessed was on Tuesday, November 16, at the auditorium of Santa Ana High School. Under the direction of William Christie, the group has recorded its version on the Erato label.

17 See James Anderson Winn, *John Dryden and His World* (New Haven, CT: Yale University Press, 1987), 448–49.

18 See Vinton A. Dearing, ed., *The Works of John Dryden* (Berkeley: University of California Press, 1996), 16:309.

19 For example, in the dedication, Dryden praises Charles II's "Clemency and Moderation," adding in parentheses, "the inherent Virtues of his Family." The reference could be to Charles I, who was certainly praised for such qualities often enough, but it must also apply to James II, advancing the argument that, were he to return to England, he would be generous and forgiving. How such a view would have been supported by James's past behavior, particularly his treatment of the Duke of Monmouth and his followers, is obvious enough.

20 *Antiquity Reviv'd: Or, the Government of a Certain Island Anciently Call'd Astreada* (London, 1693), 19, 57–76.
21 William Congreve, *The Complete Works of William Congreve*, ed. D. F. McKenzie and C. Y. Ferdinand, 3 vols. (Oxford: Oxford University Press, 2011), 1:14. Subsequent references to *The Old Batchelor* refer to this edition and are included in my text within parentheses.
22 For this attitude, see *The Town Display'd in a Letter to Amintor in the Country* (London, 1701), 15. Comparing *The Old Batchelor* to Congreve's serious attempt at tragedy, *The Mourning Bride*, the critic advised:

> Let him forsake the lofty Tragick Scene,
> And the dull Town with Humour Entertain;
> For the *Old Batchelor*, without a Plot,
> Will Live, when the poor *Mourning-Bride's* forgot.

23 John Hodges, *Congreve the Man* (New York: Modern Language Association, 1941), 30.
24 See John Hodges, *William Congreve: Letters & Documents*, ed. John Hodges (New York: Harcourt, Brace, & World, 1964), 8. Subsequent references to this work will be included within parentheses in my text.
25 D. Crane Taylor, *William Congreve* (New York: Russell & Russell, 1963), 15; and Hodges, *William Congreve: Letters & Documents*, 29.
26 See Hodges, ed., *William Congreve: Letters & Documents*, 2.
27 For this term, see, e.g., *A Modest Enquiry into the Causes of the Present Disasters in England* (London, 1690), 34. It was also the title of a poem written, "soon after the late Revolution," by Robert Gould. See Robert Gould, *The Works of Robert Gould* (London, 1709), 119–43.
28 In Hodges, ed., *William Congreve: Letters & Documents*, 151, Thomas Southerne prepared his brief statement for Thomas Birch, who was writing a brief biography of Congreve, which appeared in the fourth volume of the *General Dictionary, Historical and Critical* (London, 1736).
29 Charles Gildon claimed that it was "in nothing alter'd but in the Length" by the trio of friends. Since written versions are usually longer than the final acting version, they probably did do some cutting, but Southerne's emphasis upon the care with which the manuscript was read suggests many more revisions. For Gildon's comments, see the excerpt from *Lives and Characters of the English Dramatick Poets* (1699), in *William Congreve: The Critical Heritage*, ed. Alexander Lindsay and Howard Erskine-Hill (London: Routledge, 1989), 174.
30 William Congreve, *The Complete Plays*, ed. Herbert Davis (Chicago, IL: University of Chicago Press, 1967). In his edition of Congreve's *Complete Plays*, Herbert Davis indicates several places where he detects borrowings from Dryden's *Amphytrion* in *The Old Batchelor*. See, e.g., page 105 (note to V.i, 334–35).
31 See, e.g., the praise of William as "our Hercules" in "An Epistle to Mr. Dryden," *A Collection of the Newest and Most Ingenious Poems, Songs, Catches, etc. against Popery* (London, 1689), 4. Richard Braverman maintains that James II was also occasionally compared to Hercules, but surely no one would have mistaken the allusion to William III in *Amphytrion*. See Braverman, *Plots and Counterplots*, 182–83.
32 Of course some of the attacks upon William and Mary were entirely direct arguing that the Glorious Revolution had been a mistake and that the nation should take James back. See, e.g., James Montgomery, *Great Britain's Just Complaint for Her Late*

Measures, Present Sufferings, Future Miseries She Is Exposed to (no place or date but probably London, 1691).

33 Quoting the exact same passage twice, Borges dismisses Cervantes's meaning as mere rhetoric, while praising Menard's insight into modern thinking. See Jorge Luis Borges, *Labyrinths*, ed. Donald Yates and James Irby (New York: New Directions, 1964), 36–44.

34 Nicholas Barbon, *A Discourse of Trade* (London, 1690), especially 14, 35, 72–73.

35 For a general discussion of the ethical problems involved in a world devoted to self-interest and greed, see David Abercromby, *A Moral Discourse of the Power of Interest* (London, 1690), especially 87–118, 172–73.

36 Ned Ward, *The Miracles Perform'd by Money* (London, 1692), 15.

37 Gould, *Works*, 2:226–99. Since Gould's work was originally published in 1693, it probably appeared too late for anyone associated with the play to have read it. On the other hand, it was common for such works to circulate in manuscript. Such attitudes toward the commercial drift of England intensified. See also L. Meriton, *Pecuniae Obediunt Omnia: Money Does Master All Things* (London, 1696), especially 40–41, for comments on money and marriage.

38 For a summary of some of the schemes proposed at the time, see Defoe, "Of Banks," in *An Essay upon Projects*, ed. Joyce Kennedy, Michael Seidel, and Maximillian E. Novak (New York: AMS Press, 1999), 18–29.

39 For these terms, see, e.g., Mr. Richardson *Providence and Precept: Or, the Case of Doing Evil That Good May Come of It* (London, 1691), 20; and *A Modest Enquiry into the Causes of the Present Disasters in England* (London, 1690), 34.

40 William Sherlock, *Trimming Court Divine* (London, 1690), 19.

41 The first act contains a great deal of imagery about winds and fortune. See William Congreve, *The Old Batchelor*, in *The Complete Works of William Congreve*, ed. D. F. McKenzie and C. Y. Ferdinand, 3 vols. (Oxford: Oxford University Press, 2011), 1:32 (II.i, 30–31). Subsequent references to this work will appear within parentheses in my text.

42 See *The State of Parties, and of the Publick* (London, 1692), 12–13.

43 John Childs, *The Nine Years' War and the British Army 1688–1697: The Operations in the Low Countries* (Manchester: Manchester University Press, 1991), 203.

44 It is not Bluffe, the pretended soldier, who comments on courage but Sharper, who remarks, "There is in true Beauty, as in Courage, somewhat, which narrow Souls cannot dare to admire," 85 (IV.xi, 1). The war has its influence on the imagery of the play, especially in the mention of the artillery used in the battles and sieges.

45 See *Memoires Concerning the Campagne of Three Kings, William, Lewis, and James in the Year 1692* (London, 1693), 63–69.

46 For an example of this kind of attack upon William III, see Montgomery, *Great Britain's Just Complaint*, especially 37, 59.

47 For an general discussion of Sherlock and the political situation, see Charles Mullett, "A Case of Allegiance: William Sherlock and the Revolution of 1688," *Huntington Library Quarterly* 10 (1946): 83–103.

48 The fullest narrative about Sherlock appeared in *The Weesils* (London, 1691), ascribed to Thomas D'Urfey. An observer introduced into the poem as a visitor to the Weesil home concludes that Sherlock abandoned the "plain Principles" of the Church. See especially 13.

49 See, e.g., the broadside, *Dr. Sherlock Vindicated, or Cogent Reasons Why That Worthy Person Hath Complied with the Necessity of the Times, and Why He at First Refused It* (London, 1691).

50 See D'Urfey, *The Weesils*, 3–6. The wife in this allegory tells her husband that although conscience was a good thing, it was not important enough to deprive a family of a good income.
51 D'Urfey, *The Weesils*, 3.
52 Thomas D'Urfey, *The Moralists* (London, 1691), 13. Both this work and *The Weesils* questioned Sherlock's motives.
53 *A Short View of the Immorality, and Profaneness of the English Stage* (London, 1698), 102.
54 D'Urfey, *The Moralists*, 15.
55 See Joseph Spence, *Anecdotes, Observations, and Characters of Books and Men*, ed. James Osborn (Oxford: Clarendon Press, 1966), 1:50 item 118, 1:208 item 488.

Chapter 4

POLITICAL AND MORAL DOUBLE DEALING IN CONGREVE'S *THE DOUBLE DEALER*

In what might be interpreted as a fortunate aporia in William Congreve's *The Double Dealer*, Sir Paul Plyant expresses his horror at what he believes to be the discovery of an illicit relationship between Careless and his wife. Calling Careless "a Judas Maccabeus and Iscariot both," he thanks Providence for the disclosure.[1] He also thanks Providence, when Careless and Lady Plyant gull him into believing what the audience knows to be false—that the relationship between Lady Plyant and Careless has been entirely innocent. I want to argue in this chapter that Sir Paul's inability to differentiate between a betrayal for the sake of evil (Judas Iscariot) and righteous behavior (Judas Maccabeus)—to distinguish between good actions and bad, between traitors and honest men— is central to characterization and content in Congreve's comedy.

It is a work dominated by Maskwell, who intends to bring about a revolution in the families of the Touchwoods, the Plyants, and the Froths, to cheat Mellefont of his inheritance, and to carry off Cynthia, the woman to whom Mellefont is engaged. That Maskwell adds a dark tone to Congreve's comedy has long been recognized. What I want to emphasize here is the degree to which *The Double Dealer*, dominated as it is by a sense of betrayal, may owe some of its apparently unusual characterization less to aesthetic experimentation and more to the political spirit of the early years of the 1690s in which it was composed and performed.

That its characterization seemed unusual is obvious enough. Jeremy Collier later singled it out for a particularly vicious attack, noting, "There are but Four Ladies in this Play, and three of the biggest of them are Whores."[2] Dryden's comment on what had to be considered merely a moderate success for the playwright he was to proclaim as a worthy successor to Shakespeare[3] took in the audience's reaction to both Collier's "Whores" and their three gullible mates. "The women thinke he has exposd their Bitchery too much; & the Gentlemen, are offended with him; for the discovery of their follyes: &

the way of their Intrigues, under the 'notion of Friendship to their Ladyes Husbands.'"[4] Mellefont, the protagonist, was also attacked for being weak and gullible, a judgment in which Harold Weber has concurred,[5] and indeed in his own day, Congreve felt called upon to defend his characterization in the dedication to Charles Montague when he published the play in 1694:

> Another very wrong Objection has been made by some who have not taken leisure to distinguish the Characters. The Hero of the Play, as they are pleas'd to call him, (meaning Mellefont) is a Gull, and made a Fool and cheated. Is every Man a Gull and a Fool that is deceiv'd? At that rate I'm afraid the two Classes of Men will be reduc'd to one, and the Knaves themselves be at a loss to justifie their Title: But if an Open-hearted Honest Man, who has an entire Confidence in one whom he takes to be his Friend, and whom he has obliged to be so; and who (to confirm him in his Opinion) in all appearance, and upon several tryals has been so: If this Man be deceived by the Treachery of the other; must he of necessity commence Fool immediately, only because the other has proved a Villain? (Volume 1:129 [ll. 78–91])

Congreve alludes to the famous division between men as either fools or knaves, defending the virtue of openness and trust among friends. In defense of his characterization, Congreve points to the cleverness of Maskwell. What honest man would not be deceived by so "Cunning" a villain? As for the notion that the presence of so villainous a character in a play purporting to be a comedy almost calls the genre of the work into question, Aubrey Williams has pointed to the play's satanic imagery in treating Maskwell's villainy as if it belonged in the same category with Marlowe's Dr. Faustus;[6] and F. W. Bateson argued, "The Maskwell scenes may be pausibly excused as an experiment in 'serious melodrama', the kind of melodrama that Strindberg has perfected in *The Father*; but it must be admitted that it was an experiment that failed."[7] If the play is to be appreciated at all, Bateson continued, it must be for the remarkable sense of rhythm that informs the dialogue. But, as I will try to demonstrate, there is a context for the character of Maskwell and for the play as a whole.

Congreve wrote his play at a time when William III's fortunes in England seemed to be sinking. The Tory ministry that had come to power in the spring of 1692 was ineffectual in its attempts to govern; it was unanimously opposed to William III, particularly to his military involvements on the continent. Until

Russell's victory at La Hogue, James II was ready to make a descent upon England. The Jacobites were confident that they could succeed with as little as ten thousand men, but James had gathered twice that amount by April. An assassination plot against William by Grandval narrowly failed, and subsequent investigation suggested that Louis XIV and James II may have been directly involved.[8] The loss of English lives in the battle of Steenkerk caused general dismay, and though this encounter could have been interpreted as a victory, the Tories and Jacobites advertised it as a defeat.[9]

And treachery seemed to be everywhere. The situation seemed ripe for a new Titus Oates—someone who would claim that there was rampant betrayal at the very highest level of government, and William Fuller almost succeeded in filling that role. In the Anglican Church, William Sherlock's belated decision to accept William and Mary as God's appointed rulers appeared to many as a complete apostasy, and his defense of his actions on the grounds that submission was due to any villain who might seize the throne satisfied few.[10] In politics, Godolphin, First Lord of the Treasury, was reported to have been observed walking with a well-known Jacobite in St. James Park, at the early hours of the morning. That this Jacobite agent had subsequently met with Marlborough and Shrewsbury was also rumored. Correspondence with the court of James II seemed to amount to simple common sense as English politicians wanted some "insurance" against William's possible demise in battle or from sickness.

On the other hand, matters seemed to be going better in 1693. In that year, William III changed to a Whig ministry that operated efficiently. And the Battle of Landen on July 29, 1693, though essentially a standoff like Steenkerk, was interpreted correctly as a victory of a sort.[11] William was not out of the woods yet, but the audience that viewed the play in October 1693 might have felt a little more at ease about the permanence of the political settlement than that of a year before, perhaps enough at ease to take some pleasure in a comedy about betrayal but not so much at ease that they could enjoy it thoroughly. Congreve's play was to gain defenders during the coming years, but as previously noted, it had only a moderate success in its initial run.

If the political environment of the period from 1692 to 1693 influenced both the creation and the reception of Congreve's play, then it would surely have had a similar effect on other plays written at the time. Characters such as Maskwell should have been common enough at a time when the drama was so responsive to contemporary moods. Under these circumstances, Bateson's observations on Congreve's "experiment" would be a case of insufficient reading in the comedies of these years. In fact, this is precisely what may be discovered. Just as the comedies after the Glorious Revolution tended to reflect a new spirit of equality and openness, so the comedies written a few years later were to reveal suspicion and anxiety.

In Mountford's *Greenwich Park* (1691), Sir Thomas, described by one character as "an admirable Satyrist," attacks the entire fabric of society. He explains that he left the court not merely because of its "whoring" but also because everywhere "ther's Gaming and Perjury, Murder and Blasphemy, Divinity and Hipocrisie, running in Peoples Debts, and borrowing of Money."[12] As for the clergy, Sir Thomas argues that they are all hypocrites and that the wise will believe "none of 'em."[13] At the end of George Powell's *A Very Good Wife* (1693), the world is presented as being so deceptive that one is lucky just to hold one's own. The main figure tells the audience:

In short, the whole false World is all Deceit,

And I've made bold ev'n to retrieve the Cheat,

Think not of Losses therfore where there's none,

For all my Care was but to get my own.[14]

Cunnington and Quickwit, in D'Urfey's *The Richmond Heiress*, a work performed just six months before Congreve's play, contrive plot upon plot in an effort to outreach the other in the cleverness of their contrivances, revealing their plans to the audience in soliloquies similar to those of Maskwell. The final triumph of Quickwit involves having Cunnington arrested for treason against the government. The connection between private and public betrayal would hardly have been lost upon the audience or upon Congreve. If, as Aubrey Williams rightly observed, *The Double Dealer* is replete with religious imagery referring to betrayal, the tenor of such imagery is essentially social and, in the larger sense, political.

The transformation of politics into the complexities of *The Double Dealer* depends on the analogy of family and state. Maskwell is the lover of Lady Touchwood and seeks to marry Cynthia, the woman to whom the protagonist, Mellefont, is engaged. In these actions, he is betraying the trust of his patron, Lord Touchwood, and of his friend, Mellefont. "Jealous of a plot" (1:139 [I.iii, 11–12]) against him by Lady Touchwood, whose Phaedra-like passion for him he has rejected, Mellefont starts a somewhat cynical counterplot that includes the seduction of Lady Plyant by his friend Careless. And then, entirely on their own, the aesthete Brisk and the female poet, Lady Froth, begin an affair that betrays the trust of her husband and of the baby upon whom she pretends to dote. Congreve's analogy between the families of Mellefont and Cynthia, who have gathered together on the eve of their wedding, and a nation betrayed by self-interested politicians may have escaped conscious notice but its larger import must have been clear enough. The very use of the word "plot" might have alerted the audience of October 1693 to the possibility that some political application was possible. Even the mention of Maskwell's first name, "Jack" (1:140 [I.iii, 69]), pronounced by Mellefont in a speech praising Maskwell's honesty and resisting the warnings of Careless may have had significant resonance. Defoe was to name his Jacobite hero Colonel Jack some thirty years later. Congreve's emphasis on the powers of Maskwell, who believes that "Dissimulation is the only Art, not to be known from Nature"(1:167 [II.viii, 25–26]) and who, much in the manner as Shakespeare's Iago, confides in the audience through soliloquies, suggests that the essential milieu of the play is one in which distinguishing friend from enemy is nearly impossible.

Mellefont's greatest error is to trust probable appearances, but Sir Paul Plyant, who reads every event as a sign of Providence, makes a far greater mistake. He thinks that Providence is responsible for uncovering an illicit relationship between Careless and his wife and is equally willing to accept a Providential cause for Careless's transparently absurd attempt to explain away the obvious. His reliance upon a Providential explanation for events bears some relationship to Congreve's concerns in *Love for Love*, a comedy in which every character attempts to discover a code by which he or she can read hidden meanings or see into the future. Both are concerned with an obsessive fascination for attempting to interpret what cannot be known and with its farcical underside—an inability to understand the obvious. Whereas Mellefont blames his ill fortune on everything *but* Providence, and Maskwell mocks at any teleological interpretation of events, Providential explanation is left to one of the play's fools. The political-historical resonance is obvious enough. Questioned by Lord Froth about where everyone has been while he slept, Sir Paul remarks, "I don't know, my Lord, but here's the strangest Revolution, all turn'd topsie turvy; as I hope for Providence" (1:239 [V.xx, 5–7]). And in a rapid understanding of what Sir Paul cannot grasp, Lord Froth sees that his wife has been turned "topsie turvy" by the foolish literary critic, Brisk, under the pretense of studying the stars.[15]

These comments come at a point of time in which the role of Providence in human history was under scrutiny. Among those who applauded the Revolution of 1688, many interpreted it as an example of the intervention of Providence in the history of England. If the winds had not blown in just the right way, an English fleet might have ventured out to intercept the ships bearing William of Orange to Torbay. And had James II acted with any wisdom at all, the settlement might have been very different even after William's invasion. But among supporters of James II, such an interpretation was unacceptable. Although some retreated to the old idea that the true believers were undergoing a period of trial, many simply concluded that Providence functioned according to general laws and that the belief in particular Providence might suit better with the creed of those who followed a more enthusiastic kind of Christianity than that practiced by the majority of Englishmen.

Of course, William and Mary preferred to believe clergymen like Samuel Barton, who, in a sermon of 1692, pointed out that David had no trouble "so long as he had God and his gracious Providence of his side," and went on to interpret the Glorious Revolution and its aftermath as evidence that God was also on the side of the joint monarchy.[16] And they were doubtless pleased that William Sherlock and Archbishop Tillostson held similar views. But they probably resented the arguments of the author of *Julian*, the radical preacher, Samuel Johnson, who rejected such ideas as dangerous to the English political establishment. For him, William and Mary ruled by the very secular power of the English Constitution.[17] After all, the Sir Paul Plyants of England could easily view a Jacobite invasion of England as another act of Providence.

A puzzling aspect of the political resonances of Congreve's comedy involves his savage treatment of women. Although he was to deny the notion that one could extrapolate from the world of the play to the great world itself and turn the percentage of women in *The Double Dealer* who, in Collier's words, were "whores" into the notion of three-quarters of all women should be placed in that category, there is something to be said for Collier's general point of view.[18] The three women have very different characters: Lady Touchwood is a termagant; Lady Plyant has turned her husband into a Turkish slave; and Lady Froth writes execrable poetry and affects a profound feeling for her husband and her child. Yet they are alike in having not the slightest scruple about betraying their husbands' trust.

Now with Mary on the throne as England's only approximation to a hereditary monarchy, there seems to have been some association between the publications defending the abilities of women and Whiggish politics. If this connection was somewhat tenuous, there is little question that many Jacobites and Tories assumed the opposite stance. Dryden's undertaking the translation of *Satires* of Junvenal and Persius provided him considerable opportunity. Juvenal's savage attack on women in his sixth satire has as much political application as his innuendo about William III's possible homosexuality—a common Jacobite slander—in the "Argument of the Fourth Satyr" of Persius Flaccus.[19] As the translator of Juvenal's "Eleventh Satire," in this literary project, Congreve fell into the manner of Dryden's attacks on society, adding some graphic lines to Juvenal's account of the woman who returns to her husband's bed, still unsatisfied after a night of debauchery. Was Congreve, ostensibly a Whig, a secret Jacobite sympathizer?

Almost certainly not. Cynthia, who is more of a genuine heroine than Mellefont a hero, is intelligent, witty, and sensitive. When Congreve was with his Jacobite friends, like almost everyone else, he probably found enough to complain about the reign of William and Mary—high taxes, financial disasters, and loss of life occasioned by the war—yet the attack on double dealing in his play is certainly more applicable to the Jacobites than to any other group in the society. His cynical stance toward women seems that of a young man trying to appear worldly rather than a political statement, but the high estimation that the Jacobites, Dryden and Thomas Southerne, placed on his early comedies may have had a political ingredient of which Congreve was not entirely aware. What is most important, however, is the degree to which Congreve's cast of characters is shaped by the doubtful loyalties that distinguish the years in which Congreve's comedy was written and first performed.

2

In arguing for a particular political background to Congreve's play, have I managed to place it in so narrow a political milieu as to condemn it as a period piece, operating only in a limited time and place? Have I removed it from Bateson's praise of it as an experimental work, operating between comedy and serious drama only to condemn it as an entirely dated work? Assuredly not. In stressing the seriousness of Congreve's comedy, Bateson was still reacting to the attacks on Restoration comedy by social critics of the 1930s. Restoration drama had come under the lash of the powerful social critic L. C. Knights. Following the demands of F. R. Leavis and the Scrutiny school of criticism for moral seriousness, Knights had condemned Restoration comedy for its lack of social purpose and responsibility. Knights' criticism came during the worldwide depression, and it reached deep into the social conscience of that generation. If Restoration comedy was not the depiction of a realm as artificial as the fairy world imagined by nineteenth-century critics such as Charles Lamb and William Hazlitt and reified in the illustrations of Aubrey Beardsley, it seemed nevertheless the depiction of shallow, otiose people who were but slightly rooted in a real world of labor, pain, and suffering.

Against such views of these playwrights as essentially unserious came the arguments of Underwood for Etherege's almost philosophic stance, of Zimbardo for Wycherley's power as a satirist, of Fujimura for Restoration comedy's exploitation of a serious form of wit, and of Holland for its psychological truth.[20] I was busy attempting to show that the comedies were serious in another way—as a form of civilized play—when Aubrey Williams unveiled his famous argument for the Christian morality upon which these supposedly wicked comedies were based. Everyone had been working so hard to demonstrate that the plays were not the exercises in triviality Knights had presented that it was difficult to reverse direction in order to maintain that although the comedies were to be seen as making significant statements about life and art, they should not be regarded as religious documents—that their seriousness was of a different kind.

Williams concentrated his attention on Congreve, but his argument represented a new way of seeing the entire Restoration and eighteenth century. The era was to be viewed as much less secular than had previously been thought.[21] J. Douglas Canfield had no trouble showing that Nicholas Rowe's tragedies were thoroughly sprinkled with appeals to Providence.[22] Indeed, once pointed out, the only problem with proving these plays to be providential tragedies was the tediousness of multiplying instances in play after play. Arguing a Christian basis for the comedies, of course, had to be regarded as more difficult, but the attempt was to be made. Part of the "evidence" to substantiate this new view of literary history even resulted in enlisting a computer to evaluate the moral nature of Restoration rakes by way of providing scientific evidence that they were not really wicked at all.[23]

Replies to these arguments were of uneven effectiveness. Harriet Hawkins's attempt to argue that loading comedy with the burden of a Christian message was foolish because comedy was supposed to be fun was applauded in England but received less enthusiastically in America.[24] She followed this up with a more thoughtful article in which she questioned Williams's method of argument—more specifically, questioned if he subjected his ideas to the kind of negative evidence that a scientist might use to test radical theories. Whereas Robert Hume moved halfway in Williams's direction in revaluating his own position,[25] Derek Hughes published an article in which, through citing hundreds of sermons, he showed that there was little contemporary support for Williams's views on the theology of the period and none at all for reading comedy in the manner he suggested. What Hughes has attempted was to go far outside the texts of the comedies or of the debates over their moral nature in the aftermath of Jeremy Collier's attack on their immorality and profaneness, to the nature of Christianity itself at the time.[26]

One of the weaknesses of Williams's arguments was the attempt to apply a general model of Christian thought to a time when there was much debate over some of the basic tenets of the Christian religion. Although the debate over the Trinity did not come to a head among the Dissenters until 1718, a short-lived unification of Congregationalists and Presbyterians fell apart during the 1690s over charges of antinomianism. Refusing to take oaths of allegiance to William and Mary, some members of the Church of England became nonjurors. Deists such as John Toland, William Whiston, and Anthony Collins were questioning the tenets of Christianity itself. Aubrey Williams's achievement in attempting to rewrite literary history, then, was to show how important such religious material was to Restoration comedy—a form of comedy that very much reflected its age. During the reign of William and Mary and then of William III alone, in the hands of Congreve, Vanbrugh, and Southerne, comedy was raising profound social, moral, and political questions. Religion was part of this equation but not necessarily at the center of this questioning.

In my earlier study of Congreve, I suggested that the use of comedy for such a serious purpose might have been more a reason for Collier's attack than the "profanity and immorality" he saw in these plays. The playhouse was assuming some of the role of the pulpit, and what defender of the Church of England could accept that? Take, for example, the discussion of marriage between Mellefont and Cynthia at the beginning of the second act:

> *Mellefont*: You're thoughtful *Cynthia*?
> *Cynthia*: I'm thinking, tho' Marriage makes Man and Wife one Flesh, it leaves 'em still two Fools; and they become more conspicuous by setting off one another.
> *Mellefont*: That's only when two Fools meet, and their Follies are oppos'd.
> *Cynthia*: Nay, I have known two Wits meet, and by the Opposition of their Wit, render themselves as ridiculous as Fools. 'Tis an odd Game we're going to Play at: What think you of drawing Stakes, and giving over in time?
> *Mellefont*: No, hang't, that not endeavouring to win, because it's possible we may lose; since we have shuffled and cut, let's e'en turn up Trump now.
> *Cynthia*: Then I find it's like Cards, if either of us have a good Hand it is an Accident of Fortune.
> *Mellefont*: No Marriage is rather like a Game at Bowls, Fortune indeed makes the Match, and the two nearest, and sometimes the two farthest are together, but the Game depends intirely upon Judgement.
> *Cynthia*: Still it is a Game, and consequently one of us must be a Loser.
> *Mellefont*: Not at all; only a friendly Trial of Skill, and the Winnings to be shared between us. (1:156–57; [II.Iii, 1–22])

Having contemplated the foolish relationship between Lord and Lady Froth, Cynthia suggests that the marital relationship between men and women, as sketched out in Genesis 2:24, is inadequate to describe the approaching connection between herself and Mellefont. Then, abandoning this relationship born of the ritual joining of marriage as being frequently unsatisfactory, she offers the analogy to life as a game and, somewhat playfully, asks if they should not, as the modern song goes, "call the whole thing off." Mellefont continues the game imagery and suggests that they should not be governed by fear. Cynthia, however, points out that card games are governed by chance— something to worry about. But Mellefont moves the notion of marriage to a game of skill such as "Bowls," in which the judgment dominates. Cynthia then points out that whatever the game, one person has to lose. Mellefont ends the discussion by moving away from the game image: marriage is a "Trial of skill," after which the winnings will be shared. In demonstrating their wit, Cynthia and Mellefont reveal the possibility of a perfect compatibility of minds and hearts.

In this dialogue, Congreve provides much the same subtlety that Lévi-Strauss offered in his distinction between game and ritual. In a ritual there is the joining together of what seem to be unlike elements, in this case a man and a woman in marriage. As Cynthia indicates, the results are often unacceptable to both parties. In a game, the forces involved seem, at the start of the contest, much alike—the same number of players, the same style of uniform.[27] A tie or draw is hardly ever pleasurable in a game, but in the game of marriage, it may be the only solution to approaching a type of ritual that seemed in the 1690s less and less satisfactory. What Congreve offered his viewers and readers in this exchange was a serious consideration of what a good marriage might be, something more than a ceremony performed by a priest of the Church of England.

I still believe that the comic dramatists of the 1690s were indeed exerting moral pressure on the church. But such a view is part of a larger picture that, mainly because of the pressure that Aubrey Williams has put upon our construct of both the history and the literature of the Restoration, may now be seen in a clearer light—clearer at least for critics of the last few decades. I no longer see Congreve's *The Double Dealer* as I had seen it. I had thought Bateson's arguments convincing. The play was an "experiment" in "*serious* melodrama," an experiment that failed. He was certainly right about the remarkable sense of rhythm that informs the dialogue, but as we have seen, it was hardly experimental. Indeed, not only were there many exactly contemporary plays with cunning and hypocritical characters, but that acknowledged master, William Wycherley, had specialized in them. And Molière's *Tartuffe* had shown how a religious hypocrite could endanger an entire family.

This brings us back to the use of the concept of "Providence" within the play by Sir Paul Plyant. In the 1979 production of *The Double Dealer* at the National Theater, every time "Providence" was mentioned, the audience howled with laughter. Was this an indication of historical change? Had the very center of Congreve's serious meaning become an occasion for unintended amusement? Certainly there would have been more of an edge to the laughter in 1693, when the play was first performed, but there can be no doubt about Congreve's intention. The person who most completely finds providential meaning in the action of the play, Sir Paul Plyant, is a foolish cuckold whose wife has him swaddled in sheets every night so that there is no chance of his yielding to his sexual desires. Lady Plyant has intercourse with him only on such occasions as her affairs create the possibility that she may have become pregnant. He is willing to assign a providential cause for the revelation of what he believes to be the conspiracies that surround him, but no one else is so sure. Maskwell has a few references to Providence, certainly, but they are questioning and even sinister in their implications. What then is the play about, and to what extent can literary history determine the issue?

First of all, it is plain enough that the audience's amusement at the cuckolded husband blaming his situation on Providence would have been much the same in 1693 as it was in 1979. The audience did not need special knowledge of the "providential wind" that some religious thinkers (such as Pierre Jurieu) believed had brought William III's fleet safely to England. It is clear from the play that characters have to pay careful attention to the import of what is happening around them if they are going to thrive in the world. They cannot depend upon Providence. This is one of the messages carried in all of Congreve's plays. They have to save themselves. Mellefont is not a fool. He knows that Lady Touchwood is his enemy. He knows that the gathering of the families before his marriage to Cynthia is a situation rife with danger. If he fails to judge rightly about Maskwell, it is because he is not willing to be suspicious of everyone, because an open and trusting relationship to a friend was considered to be the sign of a good human being.

Admittedly, this is a play about conspiracies. If Maskwell's plot against Mellefont, with the design of displacing him as Lord Touchwood's heir and carrying off Cynthia, might be seen in larger terms as the Jacobite's desire to supplant William and Mary as the rulers of England through a variety of plots, such a reading need not displace the more general concept of the comic lover as needing a plot to achieve his ends—something as basic to comedy as the conspiracy of the lover in Richard Brinsley Sheridan's *The Rivals* produced some eighty years later. Careless, Mellefont's true friend, is able to perceive the sexual relationship between Maskwell and Lady Touchwood from the opening scene of the play, while Mellefont persists in his trust in Maskwell. Careless's cynicism may be a more realistic take on the world about him, but the audience was surely intended to like the more emotional Mellefont better.

This is not to deny the importance of the relationship between nation and family within the comedy. But again, the moral points to awareness in personal relationships as well as within the state. The dialogue in the fifth act between Lord Froth and Sir Paul Plyant brings all of this together. Lord Forth has just awakened and asks where everyone is, particularly his wife:

Sir Paul: The company, gadsbud, I don't know, my lord, but here's the strangest revolution; all turned topsy-turvy, as I hope for Providence.
Lord Froth: O heaven, what's the matter? Where's my wife? If if if
Sir Paul: All turned topsy-turvy, as sure as a gun.

> *Lord Froth*: How do you mean? My wife!
> *Sir Paul*: The strangest posture of affairs!
> *Lord Froth*: What, my wife?
> *Sir Paul*: No, no, I mean the family.—Your lady's affairs may be in a very good posture; I saw her go into the garden with Mr. Brisk. (1:239 [V.xx, 5–15])

The dialogue has Sir Paul brooding over the discovery of Maskwell's villainy and the viciousness of Lady Touchwood. He continues to think of the revelation of the plot, while Lord Froth somehow connects the overturning of Maskwell's conspiracy to the overturning of his wife in sexual intercourse. The use of the word "posture" might have been intended to evoke sexual postures as in the famous Aretino-Romano illustrations of sexual positions, at least in the mind of Lord Froth. And did Providence have anything to do with the unveiling of Maskwell and Lady Touchwood? This dialogue occurs just after Lord Touchwood has discovered what his wife and ward are up to.

Lord Touchwood makes no mention of Providence having a hand in the revelation of the plot at this point in the play. And the fact that Maskwell is dressed as a parson may suggest that the clergy have been playing a hand in undermining the family. After Jeremy Collier had accused the playwrights of the Restoration of profanity, the clergy became almost entirely off-limits for satire. But the lapse of such censorship brings Congreve's play in line with modern sensibilities. As we have seen in the chapter on *The Old Batchelor*, satire upon the clergy and religious hypocrisy was extremely popular. The same was still true in 1693, when *The Double Dealer* was staged. Maskwell has no difficulty using the parson, Saygrace, in his plans. He interrupts one of his soliloquies on the ease with which people may be deceived to contemplate getting Saygrace to marry him to Cynthia: "But first I must instruct my little Levite; there is no Plot, publick or private, that can expect to prosper without one of them has a Finger in't" (1:230 [V.xi, 5–8]). Saygrace is willing to obey Maskwell in everything, remarking, "You shall prevail; I would break off in the middle of a sermon to do you pleasure" (1:230 [V.xii, 8–9]). And after Saygrace promises to act with "discretion," following his departure, Maskwell notes, "It will be the first you have so served" (1:231 [V.xii, 25]). Maskwell may be alluding to some part of the past history of Saygrace about which the audience has no information, but it might also be taken as a slur upon the priesthood of the Church of England.

Congreve was furious at Jeremy Collier's attacks upon him and *The Double Dealer* in 1698, but from Collier's standpoint, Congreve was a proper target. His satire on contemporary society, particularly of society among the higher orders, is very much a caricature of the world of 1693, with its Jacobite plots, its seemingly discredited clergy, and its active literary culture. Such a depiction required a degree of realistic detail and convincing characterization. It was easy enough for Collier to pretend to understand that Congreve play represented a full view of society from which it might be possible to extrapolate a numerical formula suggesting that the three women in the play who betray their husbands was the exact proportion of women in the world who behave in this manner. Maskwell may be seen as perverting true religion by his betrayals, but neither religious concepts nor the clergy come off particularly well in this play. In May of 1692, Barthelemy de Lineière, sieur de Grandval was captured in an attempt to assassinate William III and executed on August 3. The plot seemed to involve both Louis XIV and James II, and as Stephen Baxter maintained, "the discovery caused great revulsion of feeling against the Jacobite cause."[28] The unraveling of Maskwell's attempt to undermine the family of Lord Touchwood and betray his friend as a veiled allusion to contemporary politics seemed to pass unnoticed. Perhaps it was too obvious or, more likely, the audience and its readers expected to hear from Congreve, the wit, and blinked at the more serious parts of the play.

Notes

1   William Congreve, *The Works of William Congreve*, ed. D. F. McKenzie and C. Y. Ferdinand, 3 vols. (Oxford: Oxford University Press, 2011), 1:207 (IV.ix, 12). Subsequent quotations from Congreve's writings will refer to this text.
2   Jeremy Collier, *A Short View of the Immorality and Profaneness of the English Stage*, introduction by Yugi Kankeko (London: Routledge/Thoemmes Press, 1996), 12.
3   John Dryden, "To My Dear Friend Mr. Congreve," in *Works*, ed. H. T. Swedenberg et al., 20 vols. (Berkeley: University of California Press, 1956–2000), 4:432–4. For a fuller discussion of Dryden's estimate of Congreve, see the beginning of Chapter 1 of this text.
4   John Dryden, *The Letters*, ed. Charles Ward (New York: AMS Press, 1965), 63.
5   Harold Weber, *The Restoration Rake-Hero* (Madison: University of Wisconsin Press, 1986), 104–10.
6   Aubrey Williams, *An Approach to Congreve* (New Haven, CT: Yale University Press, 1979).
7   F. W. Bateson, ed., *The Works of William Congreve* (London: Peter Davies, 1930), xxii.
8   See, e.g., Stephen Baxter, *William III and the Defense of European Liberty 1650–1702* (New York: Harcourt, Brace and World, 1966), 300–1.
9   Ibid., 303–6.
10 See Charles Mullet, "A Case of Allegiance: William Sherlock and the Revolution of 1688," *Huntington Library Quarterly* 10 (1946): 83–103.
11 For a discussion of this particular time, see Baxter, *William III*, 307.
12 *Greenwich Park* (London, 1691), 9.
13 Ibid., 31.
14 George Powell, *A Very Good Wife* (London, 1693), 47.
15 Jeremy Collier remarked sarcastically that Congreve seemed to believe that only fools believed in religion. *A Short View of the Immorality and Profaneness of the English Stage* (London, 1698), 64.

16 Samuel Barton, *A Sermon Preached before the King and Queen at Whitehall, the 27th of October. For Victory at Sea* (London, 1692), 39–42.

17 Samuel Johnson, *An Argument Proving that the Abrogation of King James by the people of England from the Regal Throne and Promotion of the Prince of Orange ... to the Throne of England in his Stead, Was According to the Constitution f the English Government* (London, 1692), 39–42.

18 Collier, *Short View of the Immorality and Profaneness of the English Stage*, 12.

19 See *Works*, ed. H. T. Swedenberg et al., 20 vols. (Berkeley: University of California Press, 1956–2000), 4:311.

20 Dale Underwood, *Etherege and the Seventeenth-Century Comedy of Manners*, Yale Studies in English 135 (New Haven, CT: Yale University Press, 1957); Thomas Fujimura, *The Restoration Comedy of Wit* (Princeton, NJ: Princeton University Press, 1952); Norman Holland, *The First Modern Comedies* (Cambridge: Harvard University Press, 1959); Rose Zimbardo, *Wycherley's Drama*, Yale Studies in English 156 (New Haven, CT: Yale University Press, 1959).

21 Williams, *Approach to Congreve*.

22 Douglas J. Canfield, *Nicholas Rowe and Christian Tragedy* (Gainesville: University of Florida Press, 1957). Canfield was a student of Aubrey Williams.

23 Ben Ross Schneider, *The Ethos of Restoration Comedy* (Urbana: University of Illinois University Press, 1971).

24 Harriet Hawkins, *Likenesses of Truth in Elizabethan and Restoration Drama* (Oxford: Clarendon Press, 1972), esp. 99–114.

25 Robert Hume, "The Myth of the Rake in Restoration Comedy," *Studies in the Literary Imagination* 24 (1983): 25–55.

26 Derek Hughes, "The 'Example Theory' and the Providentialist Approach to Restoration Drama: Some Questions of Validity and Applicability," *The Eighteenth Century: Theory and Interpretation* 24 (1983), 103–14.

27 Claude Lévi-Strauss, *The Savage Mind* (London: Weidenfeld and Nicholson, 1966), 30–31. Lévi-Strauss argues that games that end in a tie are more like rituals.

28 Baxter, *William III*, 301; Nisca Robb, *William of Orange*, 2 vols. (London: Heinemann, 1966), 2:345; William Cameron, ed., *Poems on Affairs of State*, 7 vols. (New Haven, CT: Yale University Press, 1963–75), 5:242.

Figure 3 Valentine Pretending Madness in Congreve's *Love for Love*. Detail of a painting by Robert Smirke (1753–1845). Maugham Collection, Holbourne Museum, Bath.

Chapter 5

FORESIGHT IN THE STARS AND SCANDAL IN LONDON: READING THE HIEROGLYPHICS IN CONGREVE'S *LOVE FOR LOVE*

The character of Sir Sampson Legend, along with that of Foresight, is one of the great achievements of Congreve's *Love for Love*. Both parties represent systems of thinking that are presented as antiquated and absurd. Before the entrance of Sir Sampson, Foresight has just been speculating on the possibility that his wife may be having love affairs. He begins by remarking that she is "young and sanguine," perfectly adequate descriptions at a time when the humors theory still governed attitudes toward character, but he quickly enters into theories of astrology, physiognomy, and palmistry, pointing out that she was born under the sign of Gemini and had a mole on her lip. Compared to these, her "open liberality on the Mount of *Venus*" (Volume 1: 285 [II. iii, 104–5]) would seem a direct description of her sexual promiscuity, not so much to Foresight and his naive appeal to palmistry, where it refers to the area at the base of the thumb, but clearly enough to Sir Sampson and the audience as part of the vaginal area.[1] Foresight's absurd mixture of out-of-date pseudosciences and primitive folk readings of character and events will play an important role in this comedy of readings and misreadings.

Sir Sampson's skeptical view of such matters and his tendency toward exaggeration are both seemingly based on his extensive travels, but he too is tied to antiquated systems. He complains that his son, Valentine, did not realize the powers that belonged to a father, "no Authority, no Correction, no Arbitrary Power" (1:286 [II.v, 5–6]). His dismissal of "Forgiveness and Affection" and his embrace of "Power" might seem to identify him as a wrong-headed disciple of Thomas Hobbes, who viewed the entire relationship between father and son as based on obedience to the parent. But Hobbes wrote mainly of "power," "dominion," and "sovereignty," the distinguishing factors between children, servants, and slaves.[2] Sir Sampson's "Arbitrary Power" smacks of the criticism leveled against Louis XIV by contemporaries and of John Locke's attack upon

Sir Robert Filmer's patriarchal ideas of government.³ Indeed, in addressing his son, Valentine, Sir Sampson maintains that his son is his "Slave" (1:291 [II.vii, 40]), a category based upon the freedom of Sir Sampson's choosing to engage in the act of sexual intercourse that produced him. This, indeed, is an argument taken directly from Filmer. The audience was supposed to find Sir Sampson's ideas outrageous and amusing. Locke provided the comic material for Congreve by his ironic stance in the face of what he shows to be Filmer's completely nonsensical approach to the origins of government. Congreve exposes the entire set of Sir Sampson's ideas in much the same way, then, as Locke exposed Filmer's in his *Two Treatises of Government*.⁴

In William III's England, such a belief in the power of the father puts Sir Sampson in the class of persons holding wrong and antiquated ideas of the family and the state. This is hinted at in the name "Legend." According to the *OED*, this might refer to an old tale, often with the implication of untruth such as might be found in the more exorbitant saint's lives. But a legend may also be an inscription, whether on a monument or the edge of a coin, and from this standpoint Sir Sampson fits into the pattern of Congreve's play, which, in addition to the romance plot, is very much about differing ways of reading the world. His concept of fatherhood as equivalent to the master–slave relationship and his notion of courtship as supported by claims to be one of the "Patriarchs [...] a Branch of one of your *Antediluvian* Families, Fellows, that the Flood could not wash away" (1:367 [V.ii, 25–27]) are like inscriptions from the ancient monuments of which he speaks with such familiarity, or like the hieroglyphics on the shoulder of a mummy he stole from an Egyptian tomb—forms of discourse with little meaning in the world of the young lovers, Valentine and Angelica.

1

If *Love for Love* shares with Thomas D'Urfey's *Love for Money* a contemporary London setting and a mingling of sexual desire and greed, it also has at least one resemblance to Dryden's *All for Love*. I do not mean Valentine's willingness to give up his inheritance and hopes in a mistaken despair of ever gaining Angelica's love, nor her confession of complete love for Valentine at the end. Valentine may seem as willing as Antony to surrender his entire world for love, but he is no tragic hero and Angelica shares none of the pathos of Cleopatra's situation. Congreve's comedy does, however, contain an odd body of words and references that suggest an Egyptian presence in the middle of contemporary London. There are four mentions of mummies, two references to "Aegyptian" and one each of the Nile, crocodiles, and pyramids. But these are merely part of a larger background. Congreve's real interest is not in Egyptian topography, history, or customs but in the concept of hieroglyphics—an ancient system of discourse that remained undeciphered until the nineteenth century. Congreve uses it as one of the key symbols in a comedy in which ordinary language seems no longer to convey appropriate meaning and as part of the larger notion of a world in which all of us attempt to "read" experience as a text.

In 1694, a year before the first performance of *Love for Love*, François Menestrier remarked in his *La philosophie des images enigmatique* that despite the researches of the indefatigable scholar, Athanasius Kircher, the meaning of the Egyptian hieroglyphics remained precisely what they had been—a complete mystery, the record of a language that contained meaning at one time but that was now incomprehensible. Kircher had pretended to have grasped the figures on Egyptian monuments as mysterious symbols that were open to a kind of common-sense interpretation. He even provided his own set of symbols for a dedication to his massive volume, *Oedipus Aegyptiacus*, but his student, Menestrier, concluded that "nous pouvons dire qu'ils nous ont plûtôt donné des conjectures ingenieuses que de veritable interpretations de ces misteres."[5] He classified hieroglyphics as one of many kinds of symbols and enigmas and went on to praise fables and metaphors as conveying more meaning than mere words. It was this notion—that words were often obscure compared to a language composed of pictures—that made the quest after hieroglyphics a major interest of the seventeenth and eighteenth centuries.[6] Menestrier extended his interest in symbols to include all kinds of nonverbal communication from icons to dreams. If he is far from Locke's admiration of the hieroglyphic as a more direct means of conveying meaning than words, his interests arise from the same distrust of language that informed so much philosophy at that time.[7]

That Congreve knew of Menestrier's book seems likely, but it is not central to my argument.[8] The concern with forms of language, both verbal and nonverbal, is present throughout *Love for Love*. Even the references to hieroglyphics are extremely varied in their meanings. The word is first used by Scandal in speaking of his satirical prints:

> I have some Hieroglyphicks too; I have a Lawyer with a hundred Hands, two Heads, and but one Face; a Divine with two Faces, and one Head; and I have a Soldier with his Brains in his Belly, and his Heart where his Head should be [...] I have a Poet weighing Words, and selling Praise for Praise, and a Critick picking his Pock**et.**
> I Have another large Piece too, representing a School;

> where there are huge Proportion'd Criticks, with long Wigs, Lac'd Coats, *Steinkirk* Cravats, and terrible Faces; with Catcalls in their Hands, and Horn-Books about their Necks. I have many more of this kind, very well Painted. (1:278 [I.xv, 96–109])

Scandal's "Hieroglyphicks" are like Hogarth's satirical *Royalty, Episcopacy and Law*, engraved in 1724. In such works, meaning is conveyed through emblems and symbols. These pictures are offered as a contrast to the collection of beauties in the manner of Kneller possessed by Tattle, a man who uses words almost exclusively for the purpose of trickery and deceit.

The next time the word appears Sir Sampson uses it fantastically in speaking of Foresight. Sir Sampson has been discussing his plans to pass on all his wealth to Ben by getting Valentine to sign away his right in "black and white" on the document. Foresight is concerned that the "Conveyance" has not yet been signed and is particularly anxious about the time of the signing—a significant matter within his scheme of astrology. This leads Sir Sampson to dismiss the importance of the stars, and, in turn, this insult to astrology provokes Foresight to call Sir Sampson "ignorant" (1:286 [II.v, 31]). Sir Sampson defends his wisdom on the grounds of his wide experience as he boasts of the deeds he did as he traveled around the world. The dialogue ends comically enough with Sir Sampson's hint that Foresight is a cuckold, but as it proceeds to its absurd finish, Foresight and Sir Sampson reveal their faith in their respective forms of discourse and their disbelief in that of their opponent. Foresight sees his world in terms of dreams, visions, astrology, and prophecy, and when he is with his nurse, he stoops to the most foolish kinds of folk superstitions. At the same time, he thinks that all the tales of travelers are so much nonsense. "I know when Travellers lye or speak Truth," says Foresight, "when they don't know it themselves" (1:287 [II.v, 51–52]). On the other hand, Sir Sampson has complete faith in his stories, while urging Foresight to abandon "Superstition." Both are speaking about the same world, but each sees it as a different text to be deciphered by different systems.

Only when Foresight threatens to break off the match between Prue and Ben with the statement that he would sooner marry his daughter to "an Egyptian Mummy" does Sir Sampson realize that he had better try to make peace:

> Body o' me, I have gone too far;—I must not provoke honest *Albumazar*—an Egyptian Mummy is an

illustrious Creature, my trusty Hieroglyphick; and may
have significations of futurity about him; Odsbud, I
wou'd my Son were an *Egyptian* Mummy for thy sake.
What, thou art not angry for a Jest, my good *Haly*—I
Reverence the Sun, Moon and Stars with all my heart. What,
I'll make thee a Present of a Mummy: Now I think
on't, Body o' me, I have a Shoulder of the Egyptian
King, that I purloyn'd from one of the Pyramids, powder'd
with Hieroglyphics, thou shalt have it sent home to
thy House, and make an Entertainment for all the *Philomaths*,
and Students in Physick and Astrology in and
about *London*. (1:288 [II.v, 67–69])

By this time Foresight is too interested in Sir Sampson's reflection on his wife's virtue to be concerned about secret and mysterious writings, even when "Hieroglyphicks" is used in its conventional sense for the first time to describe the characters on the mummy. But when Sir Sampson refers to Foresight as a "Hieroglyphick," he seems to be either using the term as a description of Foresight as an interpreter of hieroglyphics or suggesting that the astrologer, by his interest in the mysteries of earth and the universe, is himself a kind of mystery.[9] Certainly, Foresight prefers any mode of communication but the most obvious. He is unable to read his wife for the cuckold maker she is, but when Jeremy enters a few lines later, he attempts to read his "Physiognomy"—another language that seems to avoid simple reading and direct observation by setting up a mysterious system.

Foresight is the last person to speak directly in terms of hieroglyphics. In the presence of Valentine, who is pretending to have been transformed by his madness into the allegorical figure of Truth, Foresight observes to Scandal, "His Sayings are very Mysterious and Hieroglyphical" (1:354 [IV.xv, 51–52]). Valentine has just told Foresight that the astrologer will act as his spokesman in his utterances about the future. That the future he describes is predictable on the basis of past experience—empty churches, zeal transferred from religion to business, and the clocks striking "Twelve at Noon"—means nothing to Foresight. He sees mysteries everywhere, and in the commonplaces about human life uttered by Valentine, Foresight is willing to find the miraculous. "But he knows more than any body," Foresight tells his wife, "Oh Neice, he knows things past and to come, and all the profound Secrets of Time" (1:357 [IV.xvi, 34–36]).

Tattle immediately suggests that he knows more secrets than Valentine; when Foresight says that his experience with the art of physiognomy does not show that, Tattle says that he will not reveal them:

> Why, d'ye think I'll tell you, Sir! Read it in my Face? No, Sir, 'tis written in my Heart; and safer there, Sir, than Letters writ in Juice of Lemon, for no Fire can fetch it out. I am no Blab, Sir. (1:357 [IV.xvi, 43–46])

Such a response is an absurdity in view of Tattle's trait of revealing everything about his most intimate relationships with women while pretending to be entirely discreet. Yet the transition is hardly surprising, for the hieroglyphics of *Love for Love*—that code which cannot be discovered by even the subtlest of scholars—are part of a complex theme involving the nature of language as a mode of communication and as a mode of concealment. Everything in *Love for Love*—people, events, actions, and things—exists as a kind of text to be read or misread by the characters.

2

For the most part, *Love for Love* is an exercise in wrong reading. The play opens with Valentine "*in his Chamber Reading.*" Valentine tells his servant Jeremy that he wants to "digest" what he has read, leading Jeremy to draw the distinction between real food and intellectual nourishment. In Jeremy's view, he and his master are in need of something genuinely edible, and when he finds that Valentine plans to turn to writing dramatic satire, Jeremy recreates for his master his vision of the "Spirit of Famine," which haunts Will's Coffee House, the home of the wits. When Scandal enters, he seconds Jeremy's observations. "Who would die a Martyr to Sense," he observes, "in a Country where the Religion is Folly?" (1:258 [I.ii, 21–23]). Scandal is willing to accept a return to the direct satire of Aristophanes, but short of that, he finds the life of the modem poet futile. Valentine's problem is that he has been unable to read Angelica correctly. Like the hieroglyphics, she has kept her secret, while he has ruined himself financially to gain her affection. Valentine is willing to believe he still has a chance to win Angelica's love, but Scandal doubts it:

> Women of her airy Temper, as they seldom think before they act, so they rarely give us any Light to guess at what they mean: But you have little reason to believe that a Woman of this Age, who has had an Indifference for you in your Prosperity, will fall in Love with your ill Fortune; besides,

Angelica has a great Fortune of her own; and great Fortunes either expect another great Fortune, or a Fool. (1:266 [I.vii, 19–25])

Valentine sums up Scandal's attitude toward women as being based on the theory that it is better not to understand them, but despite such advice, Valentine, the lover, feels that he must know Angelica's true feelings. While he is acting the role of "Truth," a disguise he assumes as part of his feigned madness, Valentine presents his paradoxical view of women as impossible to understand, referring, of course, to Angelica:

> You're a Woman,—One to whom Heav'n gave Beauty,
> when it grafted Roses on a Briar. You are the Reflection
> of Heav'n in a Pond, and he that leaps at you is sunk.
> You are all white, a Sheet of lovely spotless Paper, when
> you first are born; but you are to be scrawl'd and blotted
> by every Goose's Quill. I know you; for I lov'd a
> Woman, and lov'd her so long, that I found out a strange
> thing: I found out what a Woman was good for. (1:358 [IV.xvi, 64–71])

It is Tattle who interrupts to know the solution to the riddle and finds Valentine's answer "to keep a Secret" absurd, though he is impressed with the explanation that whatever truth a woman should tell, like Cassandra, she will not be believed. Valentine's Lockean image of Angelica's mind as a *tabula rasa* is true enough to him. He finds her surrounded by fools like Tattle and cannot read beyond the "blotted" exterior surface that she reveals. But, as with hieroglyphics, there is a meaning in her mind that lies deeper than the mask of manners that Angelica wears as a protection against the predatory males of her society.

When Angelica pretends to believe that he is really mad and resists his efforts at a true and serious conversation, Valentine pursues his image of her as a kind of hieroglyphic:

> She is harder to be understood than a Piece of *Ægyptian*
> Antiquity, or an *Irish* Manuscript; you may pore 'till you
> spoil your Eyes, and not improve your Knowledge. (1:364 [IV.xxi, 5–7])

Picking up Valentine's image, Jeremy suggests that she may be like "hard *Hebrew* Books," a text to be read by starting at the back rather than the front. In suggesting that his master is beginning in the wrong place ("may be you begin to read at the wrong end"), Jeremy suggests that he will never attract Angelica by attempts at deception. Valentine responds by saying that Angelica presents a more complex problem than merely starting at the back and reading from right to left, as in Hebrew, or by simple reversal of meaning as in some other forms of discourse:

> They say so of a Witches Prayer, and Dreams and *Dutch* Almanacks are to be understood by contraries. But there's Regularity and Method in that; she is a Medal without a Reverse or Inscription, for Indifference has both sides alike. Yet while she does not seem to hate me, I will pursue her, and know her if it be possible, in spight of the Opinion of my Satirical Friend, who says,
>
> That Women are like Tricks by slight of Hand,
> Which to admire, we should not understand. (1:365 [IV.xxi, 10–18])

Valentine wins Angelica not by stratagems or words, but by a gesture. He states that nothing means anything to him if he cannot have her love and offers to sign the deed offered to him by Buckram. Angelica answers with her own gesture. She grabs the paper and tears it.

With that action, Angelica confesses her complete love for Valentine in a speech that might have come out of a romance, whether of Congreve's time or any other.

> Had I the World to give you, it cou'd not make me
> worthy of so generous and faithful a Passion: Here's my
> Hand, my Heart was always yours, and struggl'd very
> hard to make this utmost Trial of your Vertue.
> (1:387 [V.xii, 57–61])

She then reads a sermon to Sir Sampson on the way fathers ought to treat their sons and leaves him furious. But before he makes his Malvolio-like exit, he has a final exchange with Foresight. The astrologer cannot help remarking in his own jargon, "this is a sudden Eclipse." Sir Sampson, no longer in need of appeasing a prospective father-in-law, shouts out his irritation:

> You're an illiterate Fool, and I'm another. [and the Stars
> are Lyars; and if I had Breath enough, I'd curse them,
> and you, my self and every Body—Oooons, Cully'd, Bubbl'd, Jilted,
> and Woman-bobb'd at last—I have not Patience.] (1:387 [V.xii, 80])[10]

While this completes the comic exchange between Sir Sampson—with his extravagant and boastful dialect—and the astrologer that began in the second act, it also foregrounds the theme of language and reading at the very end of the play.

It should be apparent that while Sir Sampson and Foresight are the most obvious exemplars of the concept of conflicting languages, the theme is an important structural element throughout the play. One of the major divisions concerns the various types of languages used by the characters. Ben, for example, finds his imagery, proverbs, vocabulary, and songs drawn from the world of the sea entirely sufficient for grasping what he has to experience in London society. A dutiful son, he is willing to follow his father's demand that he marry Prue, but in fact he is so entirely involved with his ships, his fellow sailors, and the very idea of voyaging that nothing seems to penetrate very deeply. He is rejected by Prue, mocked by Angelica as "an absolute Sea-Wit" (1:316 [III.vi, 62–63]), seduced and then abandoned by Mrs. Frail, and scorned by his father. But if Ben seems an oddity in London society, there is nothing basically wrong with his heart or even with his mind. If he is rather easily seduced by Mrs. Frail, that is a sign of some naivete, but in *Love for Love* the power of women and the folly of men is a given fact. Ben recovers rapidly from his disappointment and is even ready to give his father some advice about women at the end.

If his language is filled with "Sea-Wit" that might belong in a nautical version of Swift's collection of "genteel conversation," with nothing said that is new or original, he speaks his mind without embarrassment and insists on honesty in everything he says. Naturally enough, in a country that, to use Scandal's words, makes a "Religion" of folly, no one appreciates him very much. He proposes to Prue in one of his typical professions of honesty and in his usual sailor's jargon:

> Nay, you say true in that, it's but a Folly to lie: For to speak one thing, and to think just the contrary Way; is as it were, to look one way, and to row another. Now, for my part d'ye see, I'm for carrying things above Board, I'm not for keeping any thing under Hatches,—so that if you ben't as willing as I, say so a God's Name, there's no harm done; may-hap you may be shame-fac'd, some
>
> Maidens tho'f they love a Man well enough, yet they don't care to tell'n so to's Face: If that's the Case, why Silence gives Consent. (1:318 [III. vii, 24–32])

But Ben has misunderstood Prue entirely. When he realizes that Prue really wants Mr. Tattle as a husband, he tells her precisely what he thinks of her by calling her a "dirty dowdy" and a "Cheese-curd." When Mrs. Foresight asks what Ben has done to make her cry, he comes out with one of his old sayings that seems perfectly calculated to dismiss any such absurd fits of sensibility: "The more she cries, the less she'll—[pee]" (1:321 [III.viii, 9]), and in the process he has a few harsh words to say for Mr. Tattle.

Ben tries his best as a lover, but the ballad of the soldier, sailor, tinker, and tailor, which seems to express his view of love, suggests a concept that is purely sexual. As he remarks after the dance of some of his sailor friends,

> We're merry folks, we Sailors, we han't much to care for.
> Thus we live at Sea; eat Bisket, and drink Flip; put on
> a clean Shirt once a Quarter—Come home, and lye with
> our Landladies once a Year, get rid of a little Mony; and
> then put off with the next fair Wind. (1:333 [III.xv, 82–86])

He finds himself approved momentarily and goes off in the hopes of dreaming about his new sweetheart, Mrs. Frail. Mrs. Foresight recommends dreaming to Scandal as well, but Scandal rejects dreaming as "the poor Retreat of a lazy, hopeless, and imperfect Lover; 'tis the last Glimpse of Love to worn-out Sinners, and the faint dawning of a Bliss to wishing Girls, and growing Boys" (1:334 [III.xv, 96–99]). Ben's retreat into dreams suggests a certain lack of awareness. Dreaming, after all, is the province of Foresight.[11] For Congreve, the world must be faced and won. Ben remains uncorrupted by the worst aspect of London society, but Congreve is willing to go only so far in praising what he must have regarded as a primitive state of existence. Prue, on the other hand, is eminently corruptible. Her country "Innocency" (for "Innocency" read ignorance) quickly collapses before the lessons of Mr. Tattle. Prue has already been upbraided for using the word "Smock" instead of "Linnen" by her stepmother, Mrs. Foresight (1:298 [II.x, 23–31]). The directness of her country speech has to give way to the euphemisms of social discourse. Tattle continues this piece of instruction in the way language may be used to conceal rather than explain by teaching Prue to communicate by saying the very opposite of what she really feels. She must not say that she can "Love" Mr. Tattle. If she did, Tattle explains, he would quickly lose interest in her:

> *Miss Prue.* Why, must I tell a Lie then?
>
> *Tattle.* Yes, if you'd be well bred. All well-bred Persons Lie—Besides, you are a Woman, you must never speak what you think: Your Words must contradict your Thoughts; but your Actions may contradict your Words.

So, when I ask you, if you can love me, you must say no, but you must love me too—If I tell you you are handsome, you must deny it, and say I flatter you—But you must think your self more charming than I speak you:—And like me, for the Beauty which I say you have, as much as if I had it my self—If I ask you to kiss me, you must be angry, but you must not refuse me. If I ask you for more, you must be more angry,—but more complying; and as soon as ever I make you say you'll cry out, you must be sure to hold your Tongue.

Miss Prue. O Lord, I swear this is pure,—I like it better than our old fashion'd Country way of speaking one's mind. (1:301–2 [II.xi, 28–41])

Miss Prue learns her lesson well, and her virtue (if it can be called that) is saved only by the Nurse's insistence on entering her chamber to chase Tattle out.

When Prue is put in the presence of Ben, she reverts to her former ways. She tries to follow the advice of Tattle, but she simply cannot endure Ben, and sooner than have him think that her silence means her consent in any way, she blurts out her feelings in a series of epithets as vivid as Ben's. For her, Ben is a "great Sea-Calf," an "ugly thing," and a "stinking Tar-Barrel."

She may want a man, but Ben will not do. And if she has to speak "plainly" against all the ideals of London society, she will do so rather than be married to someone who fails to satisfy her longings. Prue's descriptions of her feelings suggest that she lives in a continual sexual daydream:

For now my mind is set upon a Man, I will have a Man some way or other. Oh! methinks I'm sick when I think of a Man; and if I can't have one, I wou'd go to sleep all my Life: For when I'm awake it makes me wish and long, and I don't know for what—And I'd rather be always asleep, than sick with thinking. (1:376 [V.vi, 7–12])

Whatever her future may be like, whether she marries Robbin the Butler or takes on the city ways of Mrs. Foresight and Mrs. Frail, at the moment of her life that she appears in *Love for Love*, Prue is very similar to Ben. Both belong to a world in which the level of awareness is slight, in which language is simply a means of conveying direct feeling and emotion. Prue shows none of Ben's liking for proverbs, but she certainly knows her feelings. And that is all she knows. Prue's daydreams and Ben's night dreams belong to a world in which language is used without subtlety or mystery.

The ordinary world of London society is represented in the play by Mrs. Foresight, her sister Mrs. Frail, and Tattle. The sisters are introduced in a dialogue in which Mrs. Foresight upbraids her sister for making a public display of her free sex life by appearing at a disreputable Chelsea tavern and in a coach at Covent Garden. Mrs. Frail simply lies about her presence in Chelsea until the vivid evidence of a gold bodkin is produced by her sister—evidence that also reveals that Mrs. Foresight has been visiting Chelsea. The bodkin is like a decipherable hieroglyphic. It reveals everything directly. Mrs. Frail may hide behind a veil of words; she can stare her sister in the face and lie; but she cannot deny the vivid thing itself. Objects not only do not lie, but they also proclaim their meanings. Mrs. Foresight's possession of the gold bodkin reveals that she has been at the World's End too, that she is indeed a "Sister every way" (1:296 [II.ix, 53]). And just as Mrs. Frail is capable of carrying through a complete deception, Mrs. Foresight can pretend that she never had any form of intercourse with Mr. Scandal when he tries to remind her of their liaison of the previous night. Without any concrete evidence, who is to say that anything ever happened? Sex, like that other form of intercourse, spoken language, may leave no permanent trace and be subject to the same kind of lies that society expects of ordinary discourse.

Unlike Ben and Prue, the sisters are entirely aware of the use of lying in daily life; so, too, is that master of lies, Mr. Tattle. Tattle is the more treacherous because he will sometimes present false evidence to suggest a clue to apparent denials. Scandal summarizes his character well when Valentine suggests that Tattle is "a mender of Reputations" rather than a malicious destroyer:

> A mender of Reputations! ay, just as he is a keeper of Secrets, another Virtue that he sets up for in the same manner. For the Rogue will speak aloud in the Posture of a Whisper; and deny a Woman's Name, while he gives you the Marks of her Person: He will forswear receiving a Letter from her, and at the same time, shew you her Hand in the Superscription: And yet perhaps he has counterfeited the Hand too, and sworn to a Truth; but he hopes not to be believ'd; and refuses the Reputation of a Lady's Favour, as a Doctor says, No, to a Bishoprick, only that it may be granted him—In short, he is a publick Professor of Secresie, and makes Proclamation that he holds private Intelligence. (1:267 [I.x, 6–18])

In a curious way, Tattle's posture presents the same dilemma as the Egyptian hieroglyphics—a suggestion of a secret to be revealed, some suggestion of what that secret is, and ultimate doubt as to the authenticity of the solution.

Just as Tattle initially instructs Prue in the art of social lying as a means of seducing her, he tries to get rid of her by suggesting that what might be true on one day may be false the next. If he said he loved her the day before, his profession means nothing the following day. He notes that he slept since making his profession of love and did not even dream about her. Prue, of course, has spent her night dreaming of Tattle and has informed her father, Foresight, of Tattle's supposed love for her. Tattle at first tries to escape by suggesting that dreams come entirely by contraries, but Prue will not be put off by such arguments or by the idea that she should follow the ways of modern women and have a new man each night. When Foresight enters with an adjustment of his theories of physiognomy to suit Tattle as a future son-in-law, Tattle, eager to be off for his supposed marriage to Angelica, gives a Hamlet-like answer to Foresight's Polonius:

> I have no more Love for your Daughter, than I have Likeness of you; and I have a Secret in my Heart, which you wou'd be glad to know, and shan't know; and yet you shall know it too, and be sorry for't afterwards. I'd have you to know, Sir, that I am as knowing as the Stars, and as secret as the Night. And I'm going to be married just now, yet did not know of it half an Hour ago; and the Lady stays for me, and does not know of it yet—There's a Mystery for you,—I know you love to untie Difficulties—Or if you can't solve this; stay here a Quarter of an Hour, and I'll come and explain it to you. (1:376 [V.v, 30–40])

Tattle is about to go off for what he thinks will be a marriage to Angelica. She is to be disguised as a nun and he as a friar, supposedly a whim of Valentine in his madness. As it turns out, the nun turns out to be Mrs. Frail. The disguises are, as Tattle says of dreams, "Contraries"—exact opposites of the realities underneath. The mystery is indeed solved within the period promised. Tattle and Frail, man and wife, come on the stage in a state of total chagrin, having been deceived, not by words, the deceptive use of which they well understand, but by the disguise belonging to the emblematic costumes they assume—nun and friar.

The moral of the play belongs to those who have the last words: Valentine, Angelica, Scandal, and Jeremy. Poised between the fools and the knaves, they use disguise and deceit more skillfully than the knaves because they are brighter and more imaginative. And in Congreve's world, their hearts are in the right place. The play withdraws from the disguises they have used—the gulling of Trapland the Scrivener, the appearance of Valentine as Truth, Angelica's pretense at an admiration for Sir Sampson, and Jeremy's seeming interest in entering the service of Tattle—and the final conversation is held on the level of honest communication. Scandal confesses his error in thinking all women arbitrary in bestowing their favors, and Angelica is permitted a mild attack on the prevalence of misogyny among men like Scandal. She also warns Valentine against suspecting her if she shows herself excessively fond of him.

Angelica is concerned that Valentine might come to read her actions in a way that Tattle argued to be the usual method of social behavior—as a disguise to hide a contrary feeling. But Valentine assures her that her fondness will not call attention to itself because his affection will be even more noticeable:

> I'll prevent that Suspicion—For I intend to doat to that immoderate degree, that your Fondness shall never distinguish it self enough to be taken notice of. If ever you seem to love too much, it must be only when I can't love enough. (1:388 [V.xii, 100–3])

Valentine's answer is a graceful compliment and a delightful confession of his love for Angelica, but it does not solve the problem. Society would read her affectionate behavior as a disguise for its opposite, and in the character of Lady Froth, Congreve had already developed such a hypocritical woman in *The Double Dealer*, first performed in October 1693. Lady Froth appears to dote on her husband and gush over her baby, but before the play is over she emerges from the garden with the poetaster and critic Brisk, with whom she has been admiring the stars while lying on her back making love. Angelica seems to think that society reads behavior as a kind of secret code, assuming, more often than not, that the secret to the code involves a simple reversal of meaning. Thus, her behavior toward Valentine is understandable in terms of hieroglyphics. She does not act either fond or disdainful of him. Everyone, including Valentine, Scandal, and Tattle, has his theory of why she behaves with such indifference, but she will not reveal her secret until the end, when she is completely satisfied with Valentine's love for her. It is not an easy pose for her to maintain. She almost betrays her feeling when she learns of Valentine's feigned madness, but she recovers herself. And by her recovery and self-control she is able to hatch the plot that brings Sir Sampson to her as a suitor and enables her to seize and destroy the paper that Valentine signs in which he abandons all claim to his fortune.

3

What is one to make of all these references to hidden readings? A strict formalist might content himself or herself with the notion of a prevailing image that turns the text back upon itself. A deconstructionist could be satisfied with having found a seam in Congreve's text through which to offer a different text from the interpretation through romance that I gave several years ago.[12] But my tendency is to search for an historical key to Congreve's own hieroglyphic, and I would like to look more closely at the idea of scandal that runs throughout the play. The 1690s were particularly rich in gossip and scandal. After the Glorious Revolution of 1688, the Whigs spread the rumor that the son of James II was a fake—a child brought in for a false pregnancy. That scandalous story was only the beginning. Satires and lampoons that had previously circulated in manuscript were suddenly published. A large collection of such works appeared as "Poems on Affairs of State." The demise of the Licensing Act led to a rash of scandalous publications. Newspapers that had a sporadic existence before now became part of daily life, and the manuscript newsletters attached to them often specialized in gossip. The first secular divorce case was creating a stir as it went through the courts, and private laundry was all at once being washed in public. And the stage was also being accused of particular satire and lampoon. Thomas D'Urfey was forced to write a number of prefaces in which he denied reflecting on this or that person.[13] The Black Lists of moral offenders published by the Societies for Reformation of Manners were soon to be an organized and communal effort at imposing better social behavior on the population, but works like Defoe's *New Satyr on an Old Intreague*, published in 1693, used poetic satire to perform much the same purpose. Such social events, I have argued, had a major influence on *The Way of the World* in 1700.[14] I would now maintain that, in a more general way, Congreve was concerned with the same general problem in 1695 when *Love for Love* was acted.

Although this is hardly a new discovery for a play with two main characters named Scandal and Tattle, I do not know that it has ever been considered very seriously. Scandal rails and Tattle reveals secrets while pretending to be discreet; this is clear enough. What is not so clear is the way this theme ties in with the rest of the play. The quest for secret meaning governs Congreve's comedy. What Congreve does is associate the absurd quest for hidden knowledge displayed by Foresight with society's propensity to read some scandalous action behind the most normal behavior, to turn every man and woman into a hieroglyphic concealing some secret. And just as Kircher imposed his own system of meaning on the Egyptian hieroglyphics, so society tends to impose its meaning on what might be ordinary actions.

At the beginning of the second act, the Nurse is enraptured to see that Foresight has put on one stocking with "the wrong side outward." Foresight is also thrilled by the discovery:

Ha, how? Faith and troth I'm glad of it, and so I have, that may be good Luck in troth, in troth it may, very good Luck: Nay I have had some Omens; I got out of

Bed backwards too this Morning, without Premeditation; pretty good that too; but then I stumbled coming down Stairs, and met a Weasel; bad

> Omens those: Some bad, some good, our Lives are checquer'd: Mirth and Sorrow, Want and Plenty, Night and Day, make up our Time—But in troth I am pleas'd at my Stocking; very well pleas'd at my Stocking. (1:281 [II.ii, 12–20])

Foresight here as in the rest of the play turns the simplest event into a mystery to be probed and solved. His moralizing eventually reduces "omens" to happenings no more complex than "Night and Day," but Foresight wants to read these as signs and omens in a hieroglyphic universe.

Angelica appears at this moment and somehow Foresight reads the omens into the fear that if Angelica leaves the house, he will be made a cuckold. Since Mrs. Foresight has already made him a cuckold more times and with more men than Foresight can count, his fears are absurd. Angelica tells him:

> I have a mind to go abroad; and if you won't lend me your Coach, I'll take a Hackney, or a Chair, and leave you to erect a Scheme, and find who's in Conjunction with your Wife. Why don't you keep her at home, if you're Jealous of her when she's abroad? You know my Aunt is a little Retrograde (as you call it) in her Nature. Uncle, I'm afraid you are not Lord of the Ascendant, ha, ha, ha. (1:282 [II.iii, 23–30])

Although such direct statements about Mrs. Foresight's infidelities are thrown out to the astrologer by almost all the characters with whom he speaks, Foresight never grasps what they are telling him. Instead, he searches for secrets in the stars, in the faces of men and women, and in prophecies and omens.

Real scandal is usually as clearly evident as the infidelities of Mrs. Foresight or the affairs of Mrs. Frail. After Tattle has hinted at his having an affair with a "Woman of Quality" (1:269 [I.xi, 41]), trying to lure Valentine and Scandal into further inquiries, he finds himself caught as he reads Scandal's ambiguous comment on Mrs. Frail ("we all know her") as a slanderous remark. When he is accused of spreading scandal, he attempts to deny it, and then, when informed that she has claimed that she had an affair with him, he is willing to admit his complicity. But Mrs. Frail's expressed dislike for Tattle at the end suggests that Tattle is merely spreading idle gossip. At the same time, while Mrs. Frail will lie to her sister when accused of public sexual indiscretions, they are evident enough to everyone. Congreve knows instinctively that nothing is more destructive to social well-being than an abundant indulgence in scandal.

He hardly needs Freud to tell him that excessive curiosity about sexual matters is neither healthy for the individual nor for the community at large. We may assume, then, that Scandal undergoes a genuine conversion at the end. In effect his bitterness, mainly directed at women, is a product of a certain immaturity. Angelica's romantic gesture toward Valentine is actually the result of true love and mature judgment. Scandal does not offer to burn his hieroglyphic satires, but at least he learns not to generalize about women. And the worst punishment comes to the most notorious slanderer: Mr. Tattle is married to Mrs. Frail and doomed to a life of flagrant cuckoldom and equally flagrant scandal.

Notes

1 William Congreve, *The Works of William Congreve*, ed. D. F. McKenzie and C. Y. Ferdinand, 3 vols. (Oxford: Oxford University Press, 2011), 1:285 [II.iii, 104–5]. Subsequent citations from Congreve's works will refer to this text and be placed in parentheses within my text.
2 Thomas Hobbes, *Leviathan*, introduction C. B. Macpherson (London: Penguin, 1985), 253–56 (II, 20).
3 As Filmer explained, "the supreme power is always arbitrary for that is arbitrary which hath no superior on earth to control it." And again, "We do but flatter ourselves, if we hope ever to be governed without an arbitrary power; but the only point is, who shall have that arbitrary power, whether one man or many?" See Robert Filmer, *Patriarcha and Other Writings*, ed. Johan Sommerville (Cambridge: Cambridge University Press, 1991), 100, 132.
4 John Locke, *Two Treatises*, ed. Peter Laslet (Cambridge: Cambridge University Press, 1960), 169–220, especially 172.
5 François Menestrier, *La Philosophie des images énigmatique* (Lyon, 1694), p. 13. Kircher's *Oedipus Aegyptiacus* was published in 1652 and was highly influential. He was interested in Chinese hieroglyphics as well as the Egyptian.
6 For an excellent general discussion, see Madeline V. David, *Le débat sur les écritures et l' hiéroglyphe aux xviie et xviiie siècles* (Paris: S.E.V.P.E.N., 1965), especially 48–54: see also Liselotte Dieckmann, *Hieroglyphics* (St. Louis, MO: Washington University Press, 1970), 1–28.
7 William Warburton quotes a writer named Freret who had described the Chinese language as perfectly reasonable because it was written in hieroglyphics: "Il exprimoient la nature des choses qu'ils significoient: or du moins le determinoient en degisant les rapports de ces même choses avec d'autres mieux connues." *The Divine Legation of Moses Demonstrated* (London: Thomas Tegg, 1837), II, 31. See also John Locke, *An Essay Concerning Human Understanding*, ed. Alexander Fraser (New York: Dover, 1959), 2:162–64 (III, xi, 24–25).
8 Congreve had in his library a work on hieroglyphics and emblematic literature by Henri Estienne, *L'art de faire des devises, où il est traicté des rencontres ou mots plaisans* (Paris, 1645). Estienne rehearsed the theories of Philo to the effect that hieroglyphics contained "grave and serious mysteries" and that "there was a certain divine power" in them, but he seemed doubtful that anyone had fully deciphered them. See Henry Estienne, *The Art of Making Devises: Treating of Hieroglyphicks, Symboles, Emblemes, ... Reverses of Medals*, trans. Thomas Blount (London, 1650), 3. For the entry in Congreve's library, see *Works*, ed. D. F. Mckenzie and C. Y. Ferdinand, 3 vols. (Oxford: Oxford University Press, 2011), 3:500.

9 One early dictionary defines hieroglyphics as: "A dark mystical kind of writing, used chiefly in times past among the Pagan Priests and learned men of Egypt to hide their Knowledge from the vulgar sort. This writing was by making the forms of beasts and divers other figures; and could hardly be understood without exposition, or great knowledge in the nature of things." See John Bullokar, *An English Expositour* (Cambridge, 1676), sig. E6. Another suggests the word, "Hierogrammatei," for those priests entrusted with the interpretation of hieroglyphics. See Nathaniel Bailey, *Dictionarium Britannicum* (London, 1730), sig. 40z.

10 This is the fuller version of Sir Sampson's speech, which is from the first edition of Congreve's play. See *The Complete Plays of William Congreve*, ed. Herbert Davis (Chicago, IL: University of Chicago Press, 1967), 313 (V.i, 387).

11 The connection between dream and hieroglyphic may not seem immediately apparent, but Menestrier included a large section on dreams as a form of emblematic discourse in his book on hieroglyphics and symbols. See Menestrier, *La philosophie des images énigmatique*, 389–96.

12 See my *William Congreve* (New York: Twayne, 1971), 107–21. Although I would not claim any of the sophistication of the Deconstructionists in treating language, I have drawn a number of suggestions from Jacques Derrida's discussion of hieroglyphics at the end of his remarkable study of writing. See *Of Grammatology*, trans. Gayatri Spivak (Baltimore, MD: Johns Hopkins University Press, 1976), 269–313.

13 See particularly, Thomas D'Urfey, *Love for Money* (London, 1691), sigs. A3–A4v; and *The Marriage Hater Match'd* (London, 1692), sig. A2v.

14 See the first chapter of this book. See also my "Love, Scandal and the Moral Milieu of Congreve's Comedies," in *Congreve Consider'd*, ed. H. T. Swedenberg (Los Angeles: William Andrews Clark Memorial Library, 1971), 28–31.

Figure 4 Elizabeth Barry Acting in the Role of Zara in Congreve's *The Mourning Bride*. National Trust, Smallhythe Place, Tenterden.

Chapter 6

THE FAILURE OF PERCEPTION AND POLITICS IN CONGREVE'S *THE MOURNING BRIDE*

When Aubrey Williams argued that Congreve's tragedy, *The Mourning Bride*, echoed the Christian morality that was part of the English religious environment of the time, the only doubters might have been those who continued to follow Jeremy Collier's questionable attempt to show that the play was "a mere Rant of smut and profainness."[1] But it was mostly Congreve's comedies that drew Collier's attention. And it was with these works that Williams had his major task in showing an overall attention to Christian themes—a task that raised eventual objections that were overwhelming in their rejection of what amounted, by extension, to a thesis—a thesis that seemed capable of extending to all the literature of the Restoration. As Julia Stone Peters summed up the controversy, had Williams offered his argument as a corrective to seeing the Restoration as a period of complete dissoluteness and ribaldry in life and on the stage, it would have met general approbation. It was by extending his arguments to a point that would have made the Restoration into just another unexceptional period of Christian belief, little different from, say, the fifteenth or the early seventeenth century, Peters argued, that he met resistance from many of the knowledgeable scholars of the period.[2] On the other hand, *The Mourning Bride* evokes Providence often enough to leave it outside the equation.

The question about *The Mourning Bride*, then, is whether, allowing for a strong strain of belief in the triumph of a moral scheme governing earthly actions, such a scheme does not exist alongside other ways of seeing human experience that are specifically tied to the political and intellectual milieu of the time in which it was written. For example, Williams pointed out that the play is shrouded in darkness—a darkness of tombs and dungeons. Williams perceived in this a standard Christian view of the human condition, quoting William Sherlock's comment, "we live in the dark, and know not what is good for ourselves"; and again as an example of human blindness, "we are saved and made happy by what we feared." These quotations come from William Sherlock's *A Discourse Concerning the Divine Providence* (1694).[3] Sherlock's statements would have met with few objections at the time, but it seems to me that anything Sherlock had to say has to be judged in part by his contemporary reputation—a reputation clouded by his delay in taking the oath of loyalty to William and Mary and the subsequent scorn with which his explanations were greeted, along with the notion that his wife forced him to take the oaths for material reasons—a supposed yielding that made him appear ridiculous to the satirists of the time. If the refusal of the nonjurors to swear loyalty to the joint monarchy did not throw doubt upon the motivation of the Church of England, the seemingly worldly motivation of clerics such as Sherlock had to cast some suspicion upon what they had to say, even if it represented conventional Christian wisdom.

What I am suggesting, then, is that in addition to acknowledging the obvious enough Providential theme in *The Mourning Bride*, we should consider reading Congreve's play in its immediate political and intellectual milieu: I mean by this an awareness of a new epistemological consciousness pervading Congreve's world blended with the sense of a new kind of politics—a politics that involved an England governed by a king whose status had been determined by the Convention Parliament, a king who no longer threatened to shape the nation after the French model of absolutism. By the end of 1696, it was obvious that William III had brought the most powerful monarch in Europe, Louis XIV, to accept the peace that was to become the Treaty of Ryswick. William had brought England its first military victory on the European continent in hundreds of years. He had emerged from some early military defeats, from sadness at the death of Queen Mary, and from threats of assassination to admiration by a seeming majority of the people. If *The Mourning Bride* suggests the triumph of a moral scheme governing the universe, it is also very much a political triumph. Indeed, from the very beginning of his arrival in England with the help of the "Providential Wind," William's kingship had been read in these terms, both religious and political. For example, the Huguenot cleric and controversialist, Pierre Jurieu, had viewed William's triumph over James II as the direct intervention of God in the affairs of men.[4] He identified James II as the "anti-Christ" and William as the greatest person in Europe.

It takes very little imagination to see in *The Mourning Bride* the triumph of the young couple, Alphonso and Almeria, over the sinister older monarchs, as a celebration of the Glorious Revolution, by which the aged James II and his seeming dark Catholicism were replaced by a pair of Protestant monarchs, ruling by the will of the Convention Parliament. In Whig circles, James's brutal massacre of the followers of Monmouth, the "Dark Assizes," revealed the possibilities of violent repression. They had not accepted as genuine his efforts at establishing a toleration of all religions, seeing in that action nothing but a prelude to a Catholic takeover of England.

And the birth of an heir to the throne was dismissed as an imposture—a child introduced in a "warming pan" and passed off as James's true son. James' wife, Mary of Modena, seems to have been a far cry from Congreve's Moorish Zara, and his Manuel, a murderous usurper, is hardly very much like James. But in so far as they represent monarchs who should not be allowed to rule any country, they are close enough. From a Whiggish standpoint, this represented light coming out of darkness. This was exactly the way Congreve depicted William III in his poem, *The Birth of the Muse. To the Right Honourable Charles Lord Halifax*:

So from the radiant Sun retires the Night,
And western Clouds shot thro' with orient Light.[5]

William's victory over Louis XIV, manifested in the Treaty of Ryswick, only added to this image of William as the bringer of light and enlightenment.

There was also an aesthetic element in the portrayal of darkness—an element that I have dealt with previously and will only mention here.[6] Despite his success as a writer of comedy, Congreve also had claims to being a serious poet, and Julius Scaliger had set as the test of superior poetry, the rendering of darkness and by implication death and the fear of death. He used it in much the same way that Matthew Arnold was to use what he considered to be great poetry as a "touchstone" to judge lesser poets. Thomas Rymer, the most feared critic among Congreve's contemporaries, had followed Scaliger in establishing the poetry of darkness as a touchstone for artistic greatness, praising John Drdyen as the master of this type of poetry. And Congreve clearly was attempting to rival the work Dryden, his friend and predecessor.[7] The most famous scene in *The Mourning Bride* then—Almeria at the tomb—was a deliberate attempt to compete with Dryden, who has Creon in his and Nathaniel Lee's *Oedipus* consciously attempt to raise a sense of terror. In both speeches, the word "dreadful" reverberates through all the following lines. But Dryden's evocation of ghosts attempted to lend the supernatural a concrete feeling and produce a sense of terror in the audience. Congreve was more interested in exploring Almeria's psychological state as she searches for Anselmo's tomb. Dryden's Creon speaks of the horror of experiencing the role of a ghost:

The thought of death to one near death is dreadful:
O 'tis a fearful thing to be no more;
Or if to be, to wander after death;
To walk as spirits do, in Brakes all day;
That lead to Graves: and in the silent Vault,

Where lyes your own pale shrowd, to hover o're it,
Striving to enter your forbidden Corps.[8]

Congreve, in turn, writes of Almeria's response to the tombs as shooting "a Chilness to [her] trembling Heart" (Volume 2: 30 [II.iii, 14]), as communicating a sense of terror to his audience. Congreve's appeal to sensibility led to the popularity of his play into the early nineteenth century, when it was a magnificent acting vehicle for Sarah Siddons. By that time Congreve's entry into the race for being the best poet of darkness would have had some of the psychological appeal of the "graveyard school of poetry," such as Edward Young's *Night Thoughts* and the emotions evoked by Ann Radcliffe's and Charlotte Smith's heroines of sensibility as they wandered the gloomy castles of France and Italy.[9]

But most of all, darkness in *The Mourning Bride* echoes the theme that Congreve had exploited earlier in his poetry—a theme turning on the question of perception: how is it that we understand what we perceive? In the darkness of the prison to which Alphonso has been consigned, how is one to be certain of anything? And later in the play: how is the identity of the corpse to be known after the head has been removed? And I would argue that both Manuel and Zara die out of a failure of sight and identity. Disguise is certainly common enough in Restoration drama, but in the case of *The Mourning Bride*, the inability to trust one's senses is at the core of Congreve's play. Despite its happy ending, it is a tragedy of misperception. Like Shakespeare's Juliet,[10] Almeria almost commits suicide at the play's end out of a dread of experiencing life without her beloved husband, whom she believes to have been killed.

1

Congreve had experimented with problems of darkness, names, and identity as early as *Incognita*. In that novella, names are deliberately confused. Names may imply rank and wealth, but Congreve's characters based their judgments only upon what they perceive to be the real identity of the characters they encounter. This, in turn, leads to a playful encounter between characters who misapprehend the names of those with whom they fall in love. No such playfulness governs *The Mourning Bride*. An important aspect of the play is the sense of psychological trauma, of loss, pain, and death, which dominates the early scenes.[11] Indeed, the title itself seems to be an oxymoron. Brides are supposed to be happy and on the verge of sexual fulfillment. Instead, Almeria is mourning the death of Alphonso, whom she married just before they were parted, the sexual union unfulfilled. In another sense, like the famous Chekhov figure, Almeria is in a general mourning for her life—a life that promises no possible happiness, nothing but emotional pain and misery.[12]

At the beginning of the play, however, Almeria is specifically mourning the death of her father-in-law, Anselmo, who had expired after being imprisoned by her father, Manuel. Of course, she is also mourning for Alphonso, whom she assumes to be dead and with whom she had a marriage that was never consummated. Her confidante, Leonora, fails to cheer her up. Almeria rejects Leonora's notion that time will ease her sadness. And the entry of Gonsalez with his account of Manuel's victory over the Moors in Africa only depresses her further. By way of compliment, Gonsalez states that although the populace were "all Eyes" at the spectacle of the captive Moors, it was "not seen (tho' twice The Multitude should gaze) in Absence of your Eyes" (2:19 [ll. 25–26]). Although this is an elaborate piece of flattery, it contains a number of important elements. Most significant is the notion that what is not perceived by an individual leaves an experience without real existence. This would almost seem to be a view of perception to be famously associated with the views of Bishop George Berkeley, but Berkeley was born in 1685, and did not begin publishing his notions of "immaterialism" until the first decade of the next century. On the other hand, followers of John Locke, such as Richard Berthoge, were advancing somewhat similar arguments about perception during the 1690s.[13] Gonsalez's elaborate compliment was very much within the range of contemporary thought on matters of epistemology.

Not to be missed, however, is the political importance of the procession, which appears to please the crowds, with its exotic captives. Although William III had allowed a degree of celebration after the Treaty of Ryswick, it was thought that he tended to discourage the triumphal arches that some had planned.[14] The eyes and minds of the viewers represent a thoughtless pleasure at a colorful experience. On the other hand, such processions tend to conceal the violence that lies beneath warfare and conquest.

Gonsalez's compliment attempts to situate Almeria in an ideal time and space. But reality arrives quickly enough in the form of Manuel, her father, who apprehends Almeria's mourning as intended for Anselmo. Though emotionally focused on Zara, the Moorish queen, Manuel finds time to consign Almeria in marriage to Garcia, the son of Gonsalez. Interestingly enough, Manuel does not attend so much to language as to visible signs. He sees that Zara is angry at being chained, and perceives anger in the eyes of Osmyn (actually Alphonso). Similarly, Garcia and Perez are able to recognize Zara's love for Osmyn by her outward signs. Both Manuel and Zara, the monarchs who display over-the-top passions, appear to communicate less by language than by reading the emotions displayed on the faces of those around them.

The second act has the most spectacular speech in the play, a speech that attempts to describe the feeling of what Freud called the "uncanny." Almeria and Leonora are searching for the tomb of Anselmo amid the other tombs. What they experience is a symphony of expected sound amid silence and of some kind of spirit. Almeria has heard the disembodied voices of Garcia and Perez and listens to hear any further sound:

> Alm. No, all is hush'd, and still as Death—'Tis dreadful!
> How rev'rend is the Face of this tall Pile,
> Whose ancient Pillars rear their Marble Heads,
> To bear aloft its arch'd and pond'rous Roof,
> By its own Weight made stedfast and immoveable,
> Looking Tranquility. It strikes an Awe
> And Terror on my aking Sight; the Tombs
> And Monumental Caves of Death look cold,
> And shoot a Chilness to my trembling Heart.
> Give me thy Hand, and let me hear thy Voice;
> Nay, quickly speak to me, and let me hear
> Thy Voice—my own affrights me with its Echo's. (2:30 [II.iii, 6–17])

Congreve succeeds in getting all the senses, except taste and smell, involved in this speech: sound and soundlessness; sight that is painful; cold, contrasted to the warmth of a "trembling Heart"; the sense of touch recorded in the imagined weight of the tombs. This is followed by Almeria's morbid desire to

> wind me in the Shroud of some pale Coarse
> Yet green in Earth, rather than be the Bride
> Of *Garcia's* more detested Bed. (2:30 [II.iii, 24–26])

She now mingles the image of sex and the marriage bed with that of rotting corpses and will later make this more explicit as she speaks of the grave as "the Bed where I alone / Shall rest" (2:32 [II.v, 11–12]).

James Boswell was to show how, on October 16, 1769, Garrick, Murphy, and Davies objected to Samuel Johnson's high praise of this speech as being better than any individual speech in Shakespeare.[15] Johnson was to reiterate this praise in his "Life of Congreve" written many years later:

> If I were required to select from the whole mass of English poetry the most poetical paragraph, I know not what I could prefer to an

exclamation in *The Mourning Bride* [...] He who reads those lines enjoys for a moment the powers of a poet; he feels what he remembers to have felt before, but he feels it with great increase of sensibility; he recognizes a familiar image, but meets it again amplified and expanded, embellished with beauty, and enlarged with majesty.[16]

Johnson was not impressed by Congreve's poetry for the most part, but he recognized in this speech a remarkable appeal to the sensibility of the audience. In recording the objections to Johnson's argument, Boswell may have been reflecting contemporary critical judgments about *The Mourning Bride*. By the end of the century, in some quarters, Congreve's play was ridiculed as a "pantomime."[17] Indeed, some of the dramatic effects, particularly those involving the headless body of Manuel, bear some resemblance to Grand Guignol devices of the nineteenth-century stage. It certainly makes excellent use of stage effects to move the audience. But it also may be said that the second part of the speech might have been viewed as lacking in "delicacy" by Boswell's time—the standards of the end of the eighteenth century.

> Lead me o'er Bones and Skulls and mould'ring Earth
> Of Human Bodies; for I'll mix with them,
> Or wind me in the Shroud of some pale Coarse
> Yet green in Earth, rather than be the Bride
> Of *Garcia*'s more detested Bed. (2:30–31 [III.iii, 22–26])

What became the standard fare of the Gothic novel may yet not have appeared proper for the stage toward the end of the eighteenth century. The final part of Almeria's speech uses the classic rant of many serious plays of the Restoration, in which the heroine imagines herself transported to heaven where she will mingle with Alphonso's soul.[18]

The stage effect that has Alphonso rising from the tomb at her call has some of the same force of Hamlet's confrontation with his father's ghost, but here again Congreve plays on the notion of perception or its avoidance, as she begs her companion, Leonora, to shield her from her "Eyes" (2:33 [II.vi, 8]). Just as Congreve was playing with the poetry of darkness, so in this scene, he plays with the recognition scene of Greek tragedy. Except here the initial denial of recognition depends, in part, on a distrust of perception. Congreve may be drawing upon John Locke here and his discussion of sight as "for the most part, only passive; and what it perceives, it cannot avoid perceiving."[19] Almeria is terrified, thinking she is seeing a ghost. Alphonso, on the other hand, assumes that he is experiencing an "Illusion"—something that does actually exist as an idea of Almeria in his mind in the same way as dreams and vivid fictions exist.[20] He thinks that if he could continue motionless, the desirable "Form of painted Air" (2:33 [II.vi, 13]) might remain. When he realizes that she might be real, as with Almeria, we are given a parade of senses, including the "taste" of her "Breath," and when held in Alphonso's arms, Almeria finds her mind wandering to her being forced by her father to marry Garcia. These speeches form a harmonium of senses to establish the reality of their sexual longing for each other.

Congreve continues this theme of perception and its oddities throughout this scene. Almeria seems almost to complain about the way in which the sight of her husband has overwhelmed her:

That thou art here, beyond all Hope,

All Thought; that all at once thou art before me,

And with such Suddenness hast hit my Sight,

Is such Surprize, such Mystery, such Extasie!

It hurries all my Soul, and stuns my Sense. (2:36 [II.vii, 87–91])

She is shocked by the experience. Somewhat similarly Osmyn (Alphonso) complains of sight as a "Mechanick Sense" (2:39 [II.viii, 4]), which merely picks up the rays reflected from outside.[21] The eye, then, is more or less like a *trompe-l'oeil* box, reflecting whatever image comes through the lens. This contrasts with the mind with its powers of retention that can take an image, such as Osmyn's/Alphonso's vision of Almeria, and hold on to it.[22] The mind is capable of traveling through time, whether to the past or to the future. It can also surmount the experience of what is happening in the present, as Alphonso discovers, when he is so wrapped up in his thoughts about Almeria that he fails to perceive Zara entering in a fury of passions. Much of this reads like a reenactment of Locke's theories of perception, particularly the degree to which the mind can be so deeply involved in one set of ideas that it fails to attend to perceptions that might otherwise attract the mind's attention.[23]

2

At the beginning of act three, we are with Alphonso in a prison. There, he discovers a message from his father who had occupied that same cell. The experience sends Alphonso into a paroxysm of doubt about the human mind. He will eventually reject these thoughts, but he voices them anyway. Again he sees the mind as a receptor of impulses, and as humans condemned to think before the mind can will itself to reasoned thought. And reason itself Alphonso views merely as

the Power
To guess at Right and Wrong; the twinkling Lamp
Of wand'ring Life, that winks and wakes by turns,
Fooling the Follower, betwixt Shade and Shining. (2:46 [III.i, 32–35])

He eventually finds a way of rejecting these thoughts through political action, through working with Heli on a rebellion that is brewing. It would appear, then, that the way out of destructive introspection is purposeful action.

But far worse than uncurbed introspection is uncontrolled passion. Zara sees Alphonso with Almeria and is torn with anger. Even Alphonso, in his relationship with Almeria, is betrayed by his unfulfilled sexual longing for his wife. He compares the state of his nerves to being tortured on the rack. And Almeria complains of Alphonso's "too much Tenderness" (2:54 [III.vi, 41]), in the language of sensibility a coded description of excessive sexual desire. Zara, on the other hand, in her fit of jealousy and anger, utters one of the lines for which the play is still known: "Nor Hell a Fury, like a Woman scorn'd" (2:60 [III.viii, 43]). And Manuel is so furious at Osmyn/Alphonso that he cannot exert any control over his passions.

The last two acts involve the attempted murder of Alphonso, the accidental stabbing and beheading of Manuel by Gonsalez, Zara's prospective murder of her advisor Selim, and the suicide of Zara, along with the threatened suicide of Almeria and what amounts to a kind of mad scene. Almeria has visions including that of a detached head smeared with blood and a dagger reminiscent of the distorted imagination of Macbeth. She longs for death and the tomb where she believes she will find Alphonso. And before that Manuel screams out against Alphonso imagining his future sufferings: "[…] rack'd, / Torn, mangl'd, flay'd, impal'd—all Pains and Tortures / That Wit of Man and dire Revenge can think" (2:71 [IV.vii, 49–51]). Small wonder, that some critics considered Congreve's tragedy as excessive, as over the top.

As Almeria threatens to kill herself with poison, Alphonso appears and attempts to save her. But she is actually saved by her sensibility. The sight of the headless corpse of Manuel causes her to drop the cup of poison. The "spouting Veins, and mangl'd Flesh" (2:92 [V.xi, 53]) are too much for her. When she sees Alphonso, she has a difficult time thinking that he could possibly be real.

Can I believe
My Sight, against my Sight? and shall I trust
That Sense, which in one Instant shews him dead
And living? Yes, I will; I've been abus'd

With Apparitions, and with affrighting Fantoms:
This is my Lord, my Life, my only Husband;
I have him now, and we no more will part. (2:93 [V.xii, 17–23])

She has assumed that Alphonso had been murdered. She has seen what she thought to be Alphonso's headless body. Though there are no lips to kiss in a Juliet-like love death, the body itself is real enough. The apparitions she had experienced seemed also as real enough. After all, her vision of Alphonso at the tomb, the substantiality of which she had doubted at first, had proved to be real. Under these circumstances, surrounded by the horror of bodies, she accepts this new sight of the body she assumes to be Alphonso as the true presence of her husband.

That she has such a distrust of the seeming real has much to do with her situation. Mourning both Anselmo and Alphonso, her mind is turned to death and the possibilities of a spirit world. The appearances of Manuel and Zara, both characters of savage passions, cause her to further indulge in a withdrawal into her inner sensibilities. Their passionate reality makes the unfulfilled sexuality of her marriage to Alphonso that much more unnerving.

Meanwhile, the play is riddled with political intrigue. Manuel cries out against "damn'd Conspirators to take my Life" (2:70 [IV.vii, 27]) at one point, and rightly so. He is passionately attracted to Zara, but he more than suspects her love for Osmyn/Alphonso, whom he has in his power. Having overthrown the rightful ruler of Granada, Anselmo, he is naturally suspicious of plots against himself, and he finds Almeria's mourning for the dead former king as part of that same conspiracy. He has the psychology of a tyrant, trusting no one and doubting all who surround him.

Manuel's decision to go to the dungeon to confront Zara and her love for Osmyn/Alphonso is a choice filled with danger, but he is too much moved by his thwarted love to perceive it. His grim, accidental death at the hands of Gonzalez will eventually contribute to the replacement of the tyrant by the virtuous young couple. As suggested earlier, in general terms, this is the Whiggish reading of politics, with the young couples as stand-ins for William and Mary, and Manuel as James II. Having said this, it should be obvious that both the politics that followed the Glorious Revolution in 1688 and the current political events cast certain ambiguous shadows over the events of the play. For example, James II might well have felt that he was the victim of a conspiracy. He was allowed to flee the country without anything like a formal abdication. He waged war continually against William and his queen, whether by direct combat as the war in Ireland or threatened invasions before the Treaty of Ryswick. To the contrary, Manuel's death is conveniently final. Having his head cut off seems to end all possibility of a political resurrection.

At the same time, the notion of a conspiracy against Manuel had to remind the audience of the conspiratorial events of the time. The attempted assassination of William III by Sir John Friend, Sir William Parkins, and others, all of whom were executed in 1696 and 1697, gripped the nation with a sense that there were men at large who would willingly turn the nation over to France. Jacques Abbadie, who composed a history of the conspiracy, described how dismayed the people of England were at the nature of the attempted assassination:

> All *England* was alarm'd at the Surprizing News: and universal Horror was diffus'd thro' the whole nation; we trembl'd to think of the amazing Danger which human Wisdom cou'd neither have foreseen nor prevented, and were scarcely capable of reflecting upon our present Deliverance. The Conspiracy was the only Subject both of our Thoughts and Discourse.[24]

Abbadie described how the uncovering of the plot resulted in the formation of an "Association" for the preservation of King William's life.

Abbadie was among the many who commented on the three nonjuring clergymen who presided at the execution of Friend and Parkins, remarking that they "gave 'em a general Absolution for all their Sins, without obliging 'em either to confess or declare their Abhorrence of the particular Crime for which they suffered; and by such an impudent and irregular Action put a public Affront upon the Government and the Nation."[25] A pamphlet purporting to be "A Declaration of the Sense of the Archbishops and Bishops Now in and about London" lashed the three clergymen, Collier, Snatt, and Cook, stating that their actions were "to the great scandal of the Church," and disowning what they had done.[26] The first of these nonjuring clergymen named in this listing, Jeremy Collier, fired back with the claim that he had done nothing wrong.[27] But one author's reply to Collier claimed that what he did was "to sound a Trumpet to Rebellion, and Assassination" and to rouse the population.[28] Another complained that Collier saw nothing wrong with encouraging an invasion and considered Parkins a "Martyr."[29]

In discussing Congreve's response to Collier's attack on the stage in the chapter on *The Way of the World*, I will be more specific about his attitude toward Collier. At this point, I simply want to suggest a certain atmosphere that would have informed the audience of *The Mourning Bride*. Not only was the drawing and quartering of Friend and Perkins, followed by that of Sir John Fenwick, awful enough, but the pamphlets describing the abortive plot were often vivid in their description of what the assassination and possible invasion would have been like:

> That reeking in a murder'd Monarch's gore
> Could meet their brother Cut-throats on our shore.[30]

Congreve gave an audience still on edge about the assassination plot and the war, a play that reveled in blood and pain and that has a successful revolution by the best characters. That Manuel should regard the attempt to overthrow his reign as the work of "Conspirators" could not have been without its resonance for the audience of the time.

And what about the matter of perception that fills the play? The ending certainly pulls back from a vision of life as mostly vision and illusion. While she is under the control of her father Manuel, Almeria certainly experiences a world in which going through the ordinary motions of living offers little that is attractive. Her embrace of her husband at the end represents an acceptance of a new world, something like an idealized vision of what might have followed the Glorious Revolution. The setting appears to call forth a Spain of the late Middle Ages. Almeria and Alphonso do not travel through time, but for the audience of February 20, 1697, the embrace of the lovers at the end of the play represented acceptance of a world of toleration, political rights, and the freedom from absolute monarchy.

Finally, it should be noted that until Almeria drops the poison that is intended to add to the carnage of the prison cell, *The Mourning Bride* has all the essentials of a classic tragedy. Felicity Nussbaum has recently reminded modern readers of the pleasure that eighteenth-century audiences took in tragic endings, the audience weeping uncontrollably and some even fainting from their sympathetic associations with characters such as Belvidera (Otway's *Venice Preserved*) and Isabella (Southerne's *The Fatal Marriage*) roles often played by actresses such as Sarah Siddons.[31] And among the many revivals of Shakespeare, *Romeo and Juliet* (unlike *King Lear*, which retained the happy ending added by Nahum Tate) still kept the tragic ending that left the audience in tears. Indeed Congreve's play, which owes some literary debt to Shakespeare's, appears to be on the verge of a similar ending before Almeria is rescued by Alphonso. By the end of the eighteenth century the play would have lost its political immediacy, but the darkness that surrounds Almeria, the notion of living in a world of doubtful appearances would have continued to carry the implications that Congreve intended.

Notes

1 Jeremy Collier, *A Short View of the Immorality and Profaneness of the English Stage* (London, 1698), 32. See also Aubrey Williams, *An Approach to Congreve* (New Haven, CT: Yale University Press, 1977).
2 Julia Stone Peters, *Congreve, the Drama, and the Printed Word* (Stanford, CA: Stanford University Press, 1991), 226–27. It should be pointed out that British critics, such as Harriett Hawkins, were particularly notable in their disbelief. For another summing up, see Robert Markley, "Hariett Hawkins and the Criticism of the 1970s," in *Style* (Newark, NJ: Delaware University Press, 2005), 42–54.
3 William Sherlock, *A Discourse Concerning the Divine Providence*, 3rd ed. (London: William Rogers, 1702), 415, 416. See also Williams, *An Approach to Congreve*.
4 See Pierre Jurieu, *Monsieur Jurieu's Judgment upon the Question of Defending Our Religion by Arms* (London, 1689), 24–27.
5 William Congreve, *The Works of William Congreve*, ed. D. F. McKenzie and C. Y. Ferdinand, 3 vols. (Oxford: Oxford University Press, 2011), 2:296 (ll., 163–64). Subsequent citations to Congreve's works will refer to this edition and included within my text in parentheses.
6 See my *William Congreve* (New York: Twayne, 1971), 128–30.
7 See Thomas Rymer, *Critical Writings*, ed. Curt Zimansky (New Haven, CT: Yale University Press, 1956), 10–15.
8 John Dryden, *Works*, ed. Maximillian Novak et al., 20 vols. (Berkeley: University of California Press, 1956–2000), 13:157 (III, I, 41–48). Rymer chose as his example a speech from Dryden's *The Indian Emperour* (9:64; III.ii, 1–4), but the scene from *Oedipus* is closer to that in *The Mourning Bride*.
9 The full title of Young's poem was *The Complaint, or Night Thoughts on Life, Death, and Immortality*. It is clear that compared to the over-the-top emotions of the poetry of the Age of Sensibility and Romanticism, Congreve's poetry seemed cold. Elizabeth Inchbald maintained that only Sarah Siddons's acting kept a play with such artificial emotions on the stage. See Elizabeth Inchbald, *Remarks for the British Theatre 1806–1809*. Introduction by Cecilia Macheski (Delmar, NY: Scholars Facsimiles, 1990), 1–4.
10 The notes of the McKenzie and Ferdinand edition suggest the influence of Shakespeare's play at this point.
11 See Jeffrey Prager, *Presenting the Past: Psychoanalysis and the Sociology of Misremembering* (Cambridge: Harvard University Press, 1998).
12 Masha at the beginning of Chekhov's *The Seagull*.
13 Richard Burthogge, *An Essay upon Reason and the Nature of Spirits* (London, 1694), especially 87–88.
14 Gilbert Burnet's report that William did not want a procession replete with arches of triumph out of a dislike for such displays has been contested by at least one historian, but it may have been an impression current enough for Congreve to have exploited it. See Stephen Baxter, *William III and the Defense of European Liberty, 1650–1702* (New York: Harcourt, Brace & World, 1966), 359.
15 James Boswell, *Life of Johnson*, 2 vols. (New York: Oxford University Press, 1948), 1:390.
16 *Lives of the Poets*, 2 vols. (London: Oxford University Press, 1972), 2:30–31.
17 This was first offered by the satirist, Charles Churchill, in his *Rosciad*, l. 809, but repeated by a number of critics. See, e.g., *Congreve: The Critical Heritage*, ed. Alexander Lindsay and Howard Erskine Hill (London: Routledge, 1989), 237, 295.

18 See, e.g., the version of this rant in Dryden's *Tyrannick Love, Works*, ed. Maximillian Novak and George Guffey, 10:146; III, I, 312–28, and the note to this speech providing examples from similar speeches in contemporary dramas.
19 John Locke, *Essay Concerning Human Understanding*, ed. Alexander Fraser, 2 vols. (New York: Dover, 1959; reprint of 1891 edition), 1:183 (II, ix, 1).
20 See Burthogge, *Essay upon Reason*, 92.
21 See note 19. Locke argued that the eye takes in experience without the permission of the mind.
22 For a discussion of the distinction between the sensorium that was seen as absorbing experiences and the mind, see Heller-Roazen, *The Inner Touch* (Princeton, NJ: Princeton University Press, 2014).
23 Locke, *Essay Concerning Human Understanding*, 1:188 (I, ix, 9).
24 Jacques Abbadie, *The History of the Late Conspiracy against the King and the Nation* (London, 1696), 167.
25 Ibid., 191.
26 *A Declaration of the Sense of the Artchbishops and Bishopes Now in and about London*, 12.
27 Jeremy Collier, *Defence of His Absolution of Sir William Parkins, At the Place of Execution* (London, 1606).
28 *An Answer to Mr. Collier's Defence* (London, 1696), 6.
29 Humphrey Hody, *Animadversions on Two Pamphlets Lately Published* (London, 1696), 27.
30 *A Poem Occasion'd by the Happy Discovery of the Horrid and Barbarous Conspiracy to Assassinate His Most Sacred Majesty, and to Incourage an Invasion from France* (London, 1696).
31 Felicity Nussbaum, "The Unaccountable Pleasure of Eighteenth-Century Tragedy," *Publications of the Modern Language Association* 129 (2014): 688–707.

Chapter 7

POLITICS AND CONGREVE'S
THE WAY OF THE WORLD

This is an Age of Politicks. (1691)[1]

Few comedies provide such brilliant opportunities for actors to show off their talents as Congreve's *The Way of the World*. Yet however much Congreve directed his talents toward creating a comedy that would please the theatrical audience, he also turned to a number of serious and interrelated themes. At its heart, Congreve's play is very much a fable about the complexities and difficulties of family relationships. At the same time, it has much to do with the related subject of politics, reflecting considerable pessimism about the dismal contemporary political scene. I also want to argue in this essay that the play is essentially about the problems of Mrs. Arabella Fainall. Such a view is admittedly counterintuitive in that it is contrary to our sense of the play as performance. As readers and audience, we have to find pleasure in the lovers, Mirabell and Millamant, played originally by John Verbruggen and Anne Bracegirdle, and be fascinated by the villainous Fainall and Marwood, played by the most accomplished actors of the time, Thomas Betterton and Elizabeth Barry. In addition, the part of Lady Wishfort, acted originally by Elinor Leigh, can be powerful enough to dominate the entire play. By comparison, the role of Mrs. Fainall, acted by Elizabeth Bowman, had little of the theatrical fireworks of those acted by the stars of Betterton's Lincoln's Inn Fields troupe.[2] And yet the "moral" of the play, spoken at the end by Mirabell, appears clearly aimed at Mrs. Fainall's situation:

> From hence let those be warn'd, who mean to wed;
> Lest mutual Falshood stain the Bridal-Bed:
> For each Deceiver to his Cost may find,
> That Marriage Frauds too oft are paid in kind.[3]

I am not arguing that we should ignore in any way the theatrical aspects of the play. But we should pay some attention to Congreve's "Dedication to

Ralph, Earl of Montague," in which he appears to express surprise that his work succeeded so well on the stage and emphasizes the artistic elements of his comedy, comparing it to the works of the classical writers, Terence and Menander. A careful reading may allow us to focus on what Congreve considered the central concepts of his play. After all, while Mirabell's evocation of the title of Congreve's play functions as a riposte to Fainall's comment, it is followed by "'tis *the Way of the World*, Sir; of the Widows of the World" (Volume 2: 221 [V.xiii, 33–34]).

1

At the start of the section, entitled "Early Performers," enshrined in the Oxford University Press edition of William Congreve's *Works*, Judith Milhous and Robert D. Hume attempt a description of *The Way of the World* before presenting a detailed account of the manner in which the actors suited the roles assigned them. They write, "The structure of Congreve's last play pits two hard-headed, cold-blooded rakes against one another in a fight over control of a fortune. The villainous Fainall (Betterton) is thus matched against the worldly-wise but essentially decent Mirabell (Verbruggen)" (1:565). How Mirabell should be "hard-hearted" and a "cold-blooded rake" and still "essentially decent" is difficult to say.[4] As usual, Milhous and Hume do a splendid job of treating the relationship between the performers and their parts, but I cannot conceive of a less accurate summary of the nature of Mirabell and Fainall than this description of the characters who open the play with their dialogue.

It hardly seems necessary to indicate that their very names suggest the contrast that Congreve was attempting, the one, Mirabell, suggesting a character handsome in appearance, word, and deed, and the other, Fainall, with a name *almost* equivalent to Maskall of Congreve's earlier play, *The Double Dealer*, the Jacobite figure who is willing to destroy the Touchwood family to satisfy his private well-being. Indeed, it is difficult to understand how the Milhous-Hume formula applies to them at all. Mirabell has had an affair with the widow, Mrs. Languish. In what way this would make him a "hardened" rake, whether in the world of the play or in the world of the late Restoration, is difficult to say. In her book on Congreve, Julie Stone Peters notes the "sincerity" of both Mirabel and Millamant in their feelings for one another.[5] Indeed, Mirabell, frustrated by Millamant's playfulness, remarks acerbically, "I say that a Man may as soon make a Friend by his Wit, or a Fortune by his Honesty, as win a Woman with Plain-dealing and Sincerity" (2:144 [II.vi, 33–35]). Mirabell speaks with bitterness, but the relationship that Mirabell hopes for with Millamant may be extended to what Congreve would want within family relationships and, by extrapolation, within society itself.

How could this be? There have been a number of essays attempting to treat what we may call Congreve's political attitudes, most notably those by Richard Braverman, "Capital Relations and *The Way of the World*,"[6] by Scott Mackenzie, "Sexual Arithmetic: Appetite and Consumption in *The Way of the World*,"[7] and by Max Wildi, "Locke's Conception of the Conjugal Contract and Congreve's Proviso Scene in *The Way of the World*."[8] All of these essays make some excellent points, but both Braverman and Mackenzie view the politics of the Restoration as a unity, in which Congreve is still battling the wars over Filmer's theory of patriarchy.[9] Indeed, Congreve had ridiculed such a set of ideas in *Love for Love*. By 1695, among committed Whigs as Congreve was at the time, such concepts had indeed become the material of comedy— concepts to be uttered by the absurd Sir Sampson Legend.[10] By 1700, they had seemingly become irrelevant.[11] As for Wildi's view of *The Way of the World* as a scene of wills and contracts, this provides a doubtful account of Locke's theories and an excessively legalistic concept of the relationships in the play.

Comedy has always been topical, and for all its lasting values, much of what goes on in *The Way of the World* has relevance to the politics of the years immediately preceding the March 5, 1700, when it was first performed. By this time, William III was no longer the sympathetic widower of Queen Mary, the intended victim of an assassination plot, and the triumphant victor over the great Louis XIV at the Treaty of Ryswick in 1697. From a truly heroic figure— a King Arthur—as he had appeared in the poetry of Richard Blackmore, he now seemed to many like an aging, isolated monarch (the Jacobites would have said "tyrant") whose power seemed to be waning. Parliament was busy taking away the grants of land in Ireland that William had given to many of his favorites, and Congreve alluded to this in his prologue to *The Way of the World*. Commenting on the possibility of his losing favor with his audience and his realization that he could not depend upon his past reputation, he reflected a time when William's grants of land were being questioned:

> This Author, heretofore, has found your Favour,
> But pleads no Merit from his past Behaviour.
> To build on that might prove a vain Presumption,
> Shou'd Grants to Poets made, admit Resumption:
> And in Parnassus he must lose his Seat,
> If that be found a forfeited Estate. (2:101 [ll.,16–21])[12]

The Standing Army Controversy of 1697, which reduced the army dramatically and stripped William of all but somewhere between ten and seven thousand troops, had struck a blow against William's reputation and power. People seemed more fascinated by Peter the Great, who was visiting Europe and eventually, in 1698, England, than by William's interests—particularly William's fear of a new war with France. Parliament was controlled by his enemies or doubtful friends. Stephen Baxter describes William as "desperately unpopular" with the Parliament of 1698.[13] Former ministers were about to be tried before Parliament as criminals. And Louis XIV was soon to recognize the heir of James II as the true king of England; the peace brought by the Treaty of Ryswick seemed more like a cease-fire as a new war seemed to be brewing.

The theater itself reflected some of this uncertainty. Thomas D'Urfey, a strong supporter of William wrote two plays, acted in 1699, about Masaniello, the fisherman of Naples who led a mob takeover of the government. Thomas Dilke's *The Pretenders* of 1698 also has the fear of a mob. What mob was this? The mob unrest caused by famine and the change in the coinage? Or Parliament itself, which was assuming powers usually assigned to the monarch? Although it seemed aimed at Louis XIV, why did Crowne write a play about Caligula at this time? Why were some plays overtly Jacobite in their tendencies? The same suggestion of an attempted revolt against the legitimate government of William III fills Congreve's *Amendments of Mr. Collier's False and Imperfect Citations* (1698), his defense of the stage against the attacks of Jeremy Collier. I will discuss the political implications of this work later in this essay, but it is enough here to note that Congreve associates Collier not only with those plotting a Jacobite rebellion and with Masaniello leading a mob revolt but also, in his final sentence, with Guy Fawkes planning to blow up the state.

Occasional attempts to defend William III, such as Defoe's *Encomium upon a Late Parliament* (1699) and the anonymous, Whiggish *Cursory Remarks upon some Late Disloyal Proceedings in Several Cabals* (1699), decrying "Discontented Murmurers," were met with such replies as *A Just Rebuke of a Late Unmannerly Libel* (1699), which accused the writer of *Cursory Remarks* of attempting to defend "a Court that the whole Common-Wealth is sick and weary of."[14] And Richard Newman in his *The Complaint of English Subjects* (1699) addressed his work to William, stating, "Your Majesty is much abused, the Country most grievously injured, and oppressed; their Trade is merely lost, and in their Estates and Minds they are much decayed." This work was particularly severe on those who were becoming rich through graft while the "Poor" were broken "to pieces."[15] There were various complaints, such as the poem, *Money Does Master All Things* (1696), about society being dominated by the wealthy. And as we know from the complaints in various prologues, Jeremy Collier's attack upon the stage in 1698 had succeeded in depleting the audiences in the playhouses. It also succeeded in actually subjecting the actors to arrest. Congreve, who from at least 1697 seemed to be something like a literary adviser to Thomas Betterton and the Lincoln Inn Fields, could not have been happy.[16]

It may seem as if *The Way of the World* was not involved in all these events, but a large number of contemporary references succeed in creeping into the text. There is a reference, for example, to the Million Adventure Lottery, and Fainall mockingly states that he learned how to treat his wife from those notoriously cruel spouse beaters in the retinue of Peter the Great, who, as previously mentioned, visited England in 1698. The divorces of the Duke of Norfolk and the Earl of Macclesfield from their adulterous wives seem to be alluded to in Marwood's vivid picture of what a public divorce might look like. And the European travel on which Sir Wilfull Witwoud appears ready to embark would hardly have been possible before the Treaty of Ryswick in 1697. The very emphasis on money may not seem very different from that in other Restoration comedies, but it had particular resonance in a world suddenly conscious of debates over the function of money in society produced by the conflict over the recoinage that shook England in the middle of the decade. Even the Collier controversy gets a place in Congreve's play with Lady Wishfort's description of her daughter's upbringing by a tutor who delivered long lectures "against Singing and Dancing, and such Debaucheries; and going to filthy Plays [...] O, she would have swoon'd at the Sight or Name of an obscene Play-Book [...] What, a Whore? And thought it Excommunication to set her Foot within the Door of a Play-House" (2:208 [V.v, 19–26]).

I point to these contemporary references because, as I suggested earlier, Richard Braverman's interesting essay, "Capital Relations and the *Way of the World*," tended to see the politics of Congreve's play far too much as if England was still fighting the problems of the early Restoration. The villain, Fainall, childless in his relationship with his wife, is seen by Braverman as "impotent." But William III was also childless. What is one to make of that? Both Braverman and Mackenzie view Fainall as a representative of court society as opposed to the more bourgeois aims of Mirabell and Millamant. But the court of society of William III was more and more dominated by moral goals and reformation. Which court would he represent? In using the notion of reputation as a route to wealth, Fainall seems more like Sir Josiah Child manipulating the stock market by circulating false news than a patriarchal monarch dominating his world through physical force. And while Braverman's theory of "trust" as the motivating force governing Mirabell and Millamant has some merit, such a concept requires considerable amplification.

Perhaps one might begin an analysis of the basis for the relationships among the characters in *The Way of the World* by remarking on the striking similarities between this play and *The Double Dealer*. The villain of *The Way of the World*, Fainall, is not tied specifically to Jacobitism like *Jack* Maskwell (1:140 [I.iii, 69]), yet he is almost equally immoral. And the family of Lady Wishfort is just as much representative of the condition of society as is that of Lord

Touchwood. In both plays, the family is placed under siege. Fainall threatens to expose his wife as having had an affair with Mirabell. He wants full control of Lady Wishfort's money, including £6000 that should go to Millamant. It is a society in which the ongoing divorces of the time seemed to promise exposures of the most intimate kind.[17] And Mrs. Marwood pictures what public exposure can bring in conjuring up an image of the courts of justice as a public scene of shame and embarrassment such as Lady Wishfort would find unendurable. To Lady Wishfort's momentary thought about having Fainall "prove it" in court, Marwood provides a vivid description of public shame. The passage is worth repeating:

> Prove it, Madam? What, and have your Name prostituted in a publick Court; yours and your Daughter's Reputation worry'd at the Bar by a Pack of brawling Lawyers? To be usher'd in with an *O Yez* of Scandal; and have your Case open'd by an old fumbling Leacher in a Quoif like a Man Midwife, to bring your Daughter's Infamy to Light; to be a Theme for legal Punsters, and Quiblers by the Statute; and become a Jest, against a Rule of Court [...] To discompose the Gravity of the Bench, and provoke naughty Interrogatories in more naughty Law *Latin*; while the good Judge, tickl'd with the Proceeding, simpers under a Grey Beard [...] Nay this is nothing; if it would end here [...] But it must after this be consign'd by the Short-hand Writers to the publick Press; and from thence be transferr'd to the Hands, nay into the Throats and Lungs of Hawkers, with Voices more licentious than the loud Flounder-man's or the Woman that cries *Grey-Pease*. (2:208–9 [V.vi, 29–54]).

Although Lady Wishfort is horrified at this description, her daughter, who has reached maturity during the age of "the publick Press"—of John Dunton's *Athenian Mercury*, with its personal, confessional aspects, and *The Postboy* with its sometimes scandalous manuscript attachment—seems relatively unperturbed by public exposure, vowing that she is willing to "stand a Trial" (Volume II: 206 [V.iv, 52]).[18]

The good people in *The Way of the World* are those capable of true love and friendship. Fainall and Marwood, like Maskall in *The Double Dealer*, are clever and even witty. This does not prevent them from threatening to undermine the family of Lady Wishfort and (by implication) the social fabric. As Mirabell remarks, when speaking of the seeming failure of his "sincerity" in convincing Millamant, being witty would seem to be the opposite of true friendship. In both plays, those capable of love and friendship win the day. Equilibrium is restored to the family. Even so foolish a woman as Lady Wishfort, in her easily transferable love to almost any man and her fantasy of a feminine utopia, is willing to defend her daughter and eventually allow the marriage of Mirabell and Millamant.

2

In his *Manual* or *The Art of Worldly Wisdom* (1653; first English translation 1685), Baltasar Gracián cynically advised his readers that they might occasionally "play the card of sincerity." But such a distrustful attitude about how to get along in the world had undergone considerable revision by the end of the century, when *The Way of the World* appeared. The year before, 1699, was that in which Anthony Ashley Cooper, Third Earl of Shaftesbury, saw published his *An Inquiry Concerning Virtue* in which he praised "natural Affections" as needing hardly any defense. He argued that there was nothing like the "Pleasure of Sympathy," that the joys of love, generosity, and gratitude were the highest feelings for human beings, and that "the exerting whatever we have of social Affection, and human Sympathy, is of the highest Delight, and affords a greater Enjoyment in the way of *Thought* and Sentiment, than any thing Words can do in a way of *Sense* and common Appetite."[19] I am not suggesting any direct influence, but rather an atmosphere in which sincerity and sympathy were no longer terms of contempt.

Much has been made about wills and contracts in *The Way of the World*, and certainly Mirabell appears to be careful about getting even so emotional matters as his relationship with Millamant in some kind of legal form once she has accepted him. As we come to realize, the pretended relationship between Sir Wilfull Witwoud and Millamant is only a vague kind of agreement that can be easily dissolved. On the other hand, written contracts, such as that between Mrs. Fainall and Mirabell, which give control of her wealth to him, are legally binding and a protection for the vulnerable "Widows of the World." And yet, although such cautions are necessary bulwarks against someone such as Fainall, who has broken his marriage contract with his wife by taking Marwood as a mistress, the significant relationships in the play do not depend upon contracts. To a certain degree, they do depend upon what John Locke called "Trust." Peter Laslett pointed out that Locke used the word "compact" rather than "contract," in speaking of the relationship between the governors and the people, and that "Trust is both the corollary and the safeguard of Political virtue."[20] When governors violate their trust—the commitment to the well-being of the people—they may be swiftly removed.

To some extent then, we may see the relationships between Mrs. Fainall and Mirabell and between Millamant and Mirabell in *The Way of the World* as ones based on trust. But if we consider Millamant's famous line, "Well, if *Mirabell* should not make a good Husband, I am a lost thing;—for I find I love him violently" (2:187 [IV.vii, 6–7]), we find that she hopes that the trust that she has placed in Mirabell is justified. But more than that, she expresses the love that lay behind that trust. In much the same way, the trust that Mrs. Fainall has had in Mirabell, that led to her putting all her wealth in a legally binding "Trust" (2:220 [V.xiii, 25]) to Mirabell, is also based on her love for him. Seen through Marwood's envious eyes, Mrs. Fainall has enjoyed her sexual relationship with Mirabell so much—it has been so sexually fulfilling—that she can afford to be generous about Mirabell's relationship with Millamant. This is certainly a believable interpretation from the viewpoint of a Libertine, but it is certainly not the correct one.

Neither, for that matter, is Richard Kroll's view that the "trust" revealed between Mirabell and Millamant and Mirabell and Mrs. Fainall suggests a fatal decline in the direction of bourgeois morality.[21] Within the corpus of the play, we see that Fainall's adherence to self-interest leads him to abandon Marwood to disgrace, despite his passionate sexual attraction for her. Congreve demonstrates that the code of Libertinism can often be self-defeating. His characters are aware of the risks that they have taken in their reliance upon trust and love, but without these two elements society cannot survive. Seeing a kind of bourgeois "bad faith" in a play such as Sir Richard Steele's *The Conscious Lovers*, first performed 22 years after Congreve's play (though sketched out earlier[22]), might have considerable merit, but if Congreve has allowed self-interest to be modified somewhat by social values, surely no one would argue that Mirabell has abandoned self-interest as one of his guiding principles. It is that wonderful balance between emotion and self-interest achieved by Congreve in the plays after *The Old Batchelor* that is one mark of his greatness. Congreve asks us to see the relationship between Mrs. Fainall and Mirabell as genuine love on her part and affection on his. As the play shows, she knows him well. Not for a one moment does she reveal any doubt that he will act honorably toward her in the matter of her financial interests. The affection between them is a guarantee of this. If, as I suggested earlier in this essay, all of the theatrical fireworks among the female characters belong to Millamant (Bracegirdle), Marwood (Barry), and Lady Wishfort (Leigh), the moral fulcrum of the play turns on the quieter Mrs. Fainall, played by the less spectacular Elizabeth Bowman.

What of Mirabell? He was clearly attracted to Mrs. Fainall sexually and regarded her with sympathy and affection. He even relies upon her to help him in his relationship with Millamant, even though he must understand that this is difficult for her. When Mrs. Fainall thought she might be pregnant, should he have married her? Should he have done this even though he did not feel that he was genuinely in love with her? His argument about selecting

Fainall as a possible husband for her to protect her honor—someone who would not appear to be an improbable choice for Mrs. Fainall—was clearly an error. Mirabell probably valued Fainall's wit too much and did not apprehend how much damage he would attempt to do to Mrs. Fainall. Fainall has failed to function as a husband, betrayed his marriage vows in his relationship with Marwood, and attempts to ruin his wife and Lady Wishfort financially. Mirabell did not want to impose Mrs. Fainall's suppositious child upon a genuinely decent man, but even then Mr. Fainall, who might (in Mirabell's imagination) return to his wife as a somewhat chastened spirit, hardly seems a satisfactory husband.

As I have suggested, in some ways, then, this is Mrs. Fainall's play. The rendering of her situation has some of the social awareness to be found in the comedies of Thomas Southerne and is part of the ethical and political fable at the core of the comedy.[23] Although she has acted from affection and what she has considered the highest religious motives, Lady Wishfort has ruined her daughter's life. Arabella has been raised without any understanding of the relationships between the sexes. Languish, the husband chosen for her by her mother, was apparently, as his name implies, sexually feeble and inadequate. That, after the death of Languish, she should fall in love with Mirabell and have a sexually satisfying relationship with him hardly seems something that the audience is expected to condemn. And if she defends herself against her husband's charges of having had an affair with Mirabell before their marriage by lying to her mother, who in the audience would blame her for this? For all his commitment to sincerity, love, and affection, Congreve seemed to believe that, at times, lies may help to hold together families and society in general.

3

In the end, the family, for all its differences, is united, with Mirabell volunteering to bring Fainall back into the fold while Sir Wilful prepares to go on his travels. And if the final "moral" has to do with "*Marriage Frauds*," there is a larger message if the family is conceived as a metaphor for the state as it is in *The Double Dealer*. How might these final lines be read as a political moral? Let me repeat them:

From hence let those be warn'd, who mean to wed;
Lest mutual Falshood stain the Bridal-Bed:
For each Deceiver to his Cost may find,
That Marriage Frauds too oft are paid in kind. (2:223 [V.xiv, 48–51])

The chief "Deceiver" in *The Way of the World* is Fainall, whose affair with Marwood appears to predate and continue after his marriage to Arabella. Although Arabella's main reason for marrying Fainall had to do with her fear of being pregnant, there is no indication that she was unfaithful after her marriage or that she failed to be a willing sexual partner during her marriage.

On a political level, Congreve appears to be appealing for reconciliation within society of groups that had agreed to live in a kind of marriage united by the settlement accepted by the Convention Parliament of 1689. By 1700, when *The Way of the World* was performed, that relationship was under stress. If the Parliament of 1698 saw numerous factions at each other's throats, Congreve appeared to be calling for mutual respect, trust, and affection. The casting out of the Jacobite villain of *The Double Dealer* now appears relatively simple. For Congreve, an office holder under the government of William III, much had gone wrong.[24] The rise of newspaper reporters and public scandal, a foreshadowing of the socially isolated individual as portrayed in the character of Petulant, along with a seeming popular dissatisfaction with and rejection of the reigning monarch, who had stabilized the politics of the nation along Whiggish lines, all of this seemed to argue for a turn away from political life to private relationships—something similar to Claude Helvetius's future view of a society composed of small interest groups, including those united by family—a family unified by interest, affection, and trust.[25]

If the "moral" of the play may seem inadequate as an explanation for so complicated a work, I want to suggest that, as the basis of Congreve's play, the presence and importance of a somewhat expanded "moral" in the form of a compact fable should not be underestimated. Item 65 of Congreve's library was René Le Bossu's *Traité du Poëme Epique* (1675), a work that had extensive influence and was translated into English in 1695.[26] It is quoted by Congreve in his *Amendments of Mr. Collier's False and Imperfect Citations*, the reply he wrote to Collier in 1698 (3:81). Le Bossu argued that behind all important works of literature lay a kind of fable—a fable that might reduce complex literature to a relatively simple core of meaning. After insisting that the fable of Homer's *Iliad* was the same as Æsop's about two dogs who fought among themselves and allowed a wolf to devour the sheep, Le Bossu wanted to be certain that his readers understood his argument:

> We conclude then, that the Name of a *Fable*, which is given to the *Fable* of the *Iliad*, and that of *Æsop*, is neither *Equivocal* nor *Analogous*, but *Synonymous* and equally *Proper*, that all the *Qualities* which make any difference between them, do by no means affect either the *Foundation*, the *Nature*, or the *Essence* of the *Fable*, but only constitute the difference sort of it; and lastly that if a *Fable* be *Rational, Probable, Serious, Important, mix'd*

with *Divinities*, Amplified and *Rehears'd in Verse*, it will be an *Epick Poem*. If it has not these Conditions, it will be another kind of *Fable*.[27]

At one point he cleverly demonstrates how the moral of Æsop's fable of the quarreling dogs could easily be turned into the plot of a romance or given the outline of an historical novel.[28]

It is not outside the realm of possibility that Congreve was influenced by such a theory. He made a special point of quoting the couplets that constitute the "moral" to *The Double Dealer* in his reply to Collier:

Let secret Villany from hence be warn'd;
Howe'er in private Mischiefs are conceiv'd,
Torture and Shame attend their open Birth;
Like Vipers in the Womb, base Treachery lies,
Still gnawing that, whence first it did arise;
No sooner born, but the Vile Parent dies. (1:243 [V.xxiv. ll. 21–26])

Although no specific political situation is invoked, the defeat of "Jack" Maskall involves the hope that Jacobitism will devour itself. There is no direct allusion to the supporters of the family of James II. Maskall's first name may just have happened to be "Jack," but not for the audiences of the 1690s. Everyone knew who the treacherous "*Vipers*," with their "*secret villainy*," actually were.

As I suggested earlier, modern criticism would find the reduction of a play's impact to a few lines at the end to be absurd. Yet Congreve's use of a beast fable in the moral to *The Double Dealer*—that of the mother viper being devoured by its young—is probably significant here in suggesting the value of fable itself. We would find this a painful oversimplification for extremely complicated comedies. For example, in all his later comedies, it is the heroine who helps to unravel the actions of the villainous figures, and this is reflected in the moral of *Love for Love*, suggesting that the wonder lies in finding a "Lover true" rather than that "a Woman's Kind" (1:389 [V.xii, 126]). Yet no one would argue that such a conclusion provides a complete clue to the complexities of Congreve's play. And to complicate matters, both *The Double Dealer* and *The Way of the World* take on even more difficult subjects. Nevertheless, we should not dismiss what was probably an operative aspect of Congreve's approach to the drama.

In his *Amendments of Mr. Collier's False and Imperfect Citations*, Congreve defends the purpose of these "morals" at the end of his plays. He writes,

There is generally Care taken, that the Moral of the whole shall be summ'd up, and deliver'd to the Audience, in the very last and concluding

Lines of the Poem. The Intention of this is, that the Delight of the Representation may not so strongly possess the Minds of the Audience, as to make them forget or oversee the Instruction: It is the last thing said, that it may make the last Impression; and it is always comprehended in a few Lines, and put into Rhyme, that it may be easy and engaging to the Memory. (3:79–80 [179–88])

Although this attempt to separate the experience of the whole performance, whether seen or read, is out of keeping with modern critical concepts, Congreve's argument was certainly in keeping with contemporary critical theory, which emphasized separate rhetorical modes rather than an organic whole. Just a few years later, George Farquhar, alluding to Æsop's fables, was to argue that comedy is no more at present than a "well-fram'd Tale handsomely told, as an agreeable Vehicle for Counsel or Reproof."[29] Farquhar may have been deliberately paradoxical, when he argued that the only difference between modern stage comedy and one of Aesop's fables was that Aesop's fables were shorter. On the other hand, he pointed to the episode in Congreve's *The Old Batchelor*, involving Fondlewife and his "young Spouse," as being essentially the same as Æsop's fable of the "*Eagle* and Cockle."[30] In other words, at a time when the beast fable was amazingly popular, Farquhar saw no disadvantage in comparing a critically accepted genre such as stage comedy with a form frequently involving talking animals.[31] This concept of fable also has the advantage of supporting my earlier contention about Mrs. Fainall's situation being at the "heart" of the play. And surely having made such a full argument for the importance of the "moral" in his *Amendments*, just two years earlier, he would have been especially careful in writing it.

There also appears to be a larger fable in *The Way of the World* alluded to in the concluding "moral" that may be read from the standpoint of ethics and history. The ethical import of the play is clear enough. Lady Wishfort, through her puritanical upbringing of her daughter, Arabella, nearly succeeded in destroying her life. Her marriage to Languish was clearly a disaster, leaving her sexually unfulfilled. Arabella's relationship with Mirabell involved true love on her part, but the danger of having a child led to her marriage to Fainall, whose subsequent adulterous affair with Marwood leads to Arabella's unhappiness at the start of the play.[32] Fainall, who is capable of some amusement at learning of Arabella's affair with Mirabell prior to their marriage, reveals his true, Libertine colors. She was, after all, before her marriage, a widow of independent means, free to choose the kind of life she wished to lead. But Fainall, in pretending to moral indignation, chooses to act the part of a hypocrite. Defeated by his wife and her trust in Mirabell, Fainall actually draws his sword and attempts to kill his wife, a loss of control that suggests a degree of emotional weakness. He leaves the scene, bitter and defeated. Mirabell thinks that Fainall may now make an acceptable husband. But Mrs. Fainall seems to be happy to be rid of him. Those capable of genuine love and affection—Mrs. Fainall, Mirabell, and Millamant—emerge triumphant, with the latter couple establishing a world of true understanding and sympathy. The hypocrisy of Lady Wishfort, with her embarrassing sexual longings, is to be laughed at and perhaps pitied to some extent; but the vicious hypocrisy of Marwood is recognized and rejected by everyone, and the moral hypocrisy of Fainall, along with his desire for wealth and power, are scorned by all.

Such a story may also be given a much richer meaning if the fable is given an expanded reading along historical and political lines. Although I have tried to emphasize the way Congreve's play reflects the exact contemporary scene, this does not mean that he lacked an interest in historical events and what he considered their import. Lady Wishfort represents the puritanical streak in the nation. It had triumphed during the interregnum, a period that saw the shutting down of a once flourishing theatrical scene. When she puts Marwood into her closet, she lists the reading material available: "Dear Friend retire into my Closet, that I may examine [Mrs. Fainall] with more Freedom [...] There are Books over the Chimney—Quarles and Pryn, and the *Short View of the Stage* [by Jeremy Collier], with *Bunyan's* Works to entertain you" (2:151 [III.v, 19–23]). Lady Wishfort's library nicely joins works of the puritanical interregnum with its anti-theatrical bias accompanied by more modern works of the same flavor. The attitudes of this earlier period continued to exist even while they were displaced from power at the Restoration. It was followed by a period in which Libertinism was indeed the mode of the court of Charles II. Mirabell's affair with the widow, Arabella Languish, would have to be viewed as the kind of relationship, which, if carried on with discretion, would have brought little condemnation at a time when, in Europe, the prevalence of mistresses among the upper orders was inspiring an entire line of property laws devoted to concubines. The relationship was satisfying to a certain extent for both Mirabell and Arabella. It partly made up for the puritanical upbringing by Arabella's mother that had distorted her life, but since Mirabell was not genuinely in love with her, it was not wholly satisfactory. And with the threat of a pregnancy, it resulted in the marriage to Fainall—a marriage that proved less than adequate as he emerged as an adulterous husband. His attempt to take over financial control of the family is defeated by Mrs. Fainall's entire trust in Mirabell—a trust born of her love. Similarly, James II, who like Fainall had a legitimate claim to be the head of the family (state), tried to impose his will upon England in the form of his Catholicism, disguised under a claim of freedom of conscience. Just as James was defeated in his attempt by William III, who ruled the nation through his love for his people and his refusal to be deceived by forces still loyal to James, so Fainall, like the Jacobites, remains exiled, embittered, and filled with the delusion that he might yet return to power.

Not all the parts fit in this reductive political reading of the play as an historical fable, but it is still possible to make this operate as a general pattern offering a Whiggish myth. For example, Jeremy Collier was actually a nonjuror, who, on April 3, 1696, had acted as a priest at the scaffold in absolving Sir John Friend and Sir William Perkyns of having sinned in their effort at assassinating William III. Of course, as has been seen, he was also the author of the *Short View of the Immorality and Profaneness of the English Stage* in 1698, an attack that had brought the stage into disrepute and which had involved Congreve in a nasty exchange with Collier. To more than a few contemporaries, Collier's attack upon the stage seemed to be a revival of the puritanical attack on the theater by William Prynne during the interregnum.[33] For example, John Dennis suggested that Collier's absolving of Friend and Perkyns had brought England close to "another Civil War."[34]

Within Congreve's play, the war upon art and the theater is mainly born by Lady Wishfort in her theories of education and in the reading material in her library, which includes Collier's attack. But we should remember that, as hypocritical as it may be, Fainall's attempt to bring his wife to her knees is based on her supposed immorality—her having had an affair with Mirabell before their marriage and his seeming insistence upon making it public. He is willing to bet on Lady Wishfort's horror of scandal, and even if his action destroys Marwood's reputation and makes public his own having been made a cuckold in embryo by his wife, he appears willing to sacrifice all to his supposed moral indignation. His hypocritical accusation is not very different from the way Congreve and his fellow playwrights viewed Collier's combination of seeming moral dudgeon in his attacks upon the theater and his actual attempts to subvert the political basis of society in seeming to encourage the destruction of the kind of government that William III had brought to England by the events of 1688 and 1689.[35]

Much of this weaving together of politics and the drama emerges in Congreve's reply to Jeremy Collier. Because Collier's attack has almost always been treated mainly as a challenge to the moral validity of Restoration comedy, Congreve's reply has always been faulted as an inadequate response to Collier's claim to the moral high ground.[36] I want to suggest that it should be viewed not so much as a document in the history of aesthetics or the history of the drama but rather as a rejoinder to what Congreve saw as Collier's political aims —and that this occurs from the very beginning of the work. Although Congreve attempts to explain the purposes of stage comedy in response to Collier's arguments, he states over and over again that Collier is completely out of his depth as a literary critic—that on matters of literary criticism, he is not worth answering. Where Collier represents a danger is as someone putting forward reactionary political concepts, which, by subverting the function of the stage in contemporary society, aim at destroying an institution that provides a necessary amusement to the restive English temperament. After pointing to the frequency of suicides in England, he concludes,

> From whence are all our Sects, Schisms, and innumerable Subdivisions in Religion? Whence our Plots, Conspiracies, and Seditions? Who are the Authors and Contrivers of these things? Not they who frequent the Theatres and Consorts of Musick. No, if they had, it may be Mr. *Collier's* Invective had not been levell'd that way; his *Gun-Powder-Treason* Plot upon Musick and Plays (for he says *Musick is as dangerous as Gun-Powder*) had broke out in another Place, and all his False-Witnesses had been summoned elsewhere. (3:124 [ll. 1818–27])

In Congreve's mind, Jeremy Collier's chief purpose in his *Short View* is a seditious plot against the social and political structure of William III's England. At one point he notes Collier's approbation of Cicero's belief that the same person should be in charge of both the state and of religion in the nation. Congreve asks, "What does he mean by this? What Occasion is there of this Quotation, in our Country? Is not our King both at the Head of our Religion and Government? When Mr. *Collier* allows him one, perhaps he will not deny him the other" (3:103–4 [ll. 1063–67]). Congreve's entire pattern of defense is notably based on Whiggish principles. He demands the right of *habeas corpus* as the justification for defending himself against Collier's attacks. And he frequently points to his right to satirize members of the upper orders of society as he does in his *The Double Dealer*. He views Collier, on the other hand, as someone committed to a system of absolute rule through a monarch and reverence for the aristocracy. He notes that Collier writes more "like a Herald-Painter than a Priest" (3:103 [l. 1045]).

To Congreve's way of thinking, Collier remains the Jacobite who gave a spiritual pardon to those who were trying to assassinate William III. The comparison to Guy Fawkes that he makes, then, would not have seemed at all far-fetched given Congreve's patterns of association. The attempt to destroy all theatrical and musical performance in England (and this, not simply reformation, was indeed Collier's goal) appeared little different from Guy Fawkes's attempt to blow up the Parliament. And in speaking of Collier's "Zeal" (3:113 [l.1402, 1407]), a word always associated with the Puritans and their war against the theater, he links the Jacobite cause to that of William Prynne, whose *Historio-mastix* (1633) provided the moral argument against the stage that kept the theaters closed during the interregnum. For Congreve this link finds a place in the character of the priest, Mathan, from Racine's *Athalie*, whom Collier praises despite Mathan's turn to worshipping Baal. Congreve turns this into Collier's admiration for a priest, who is willing to revolt against the established order.

In arguing, then, as I have previously, that Congreve's *Way of the World* was Congreve's fullest reply to Collier, I did so on the grounds that he created in the worldly sophistication of both Mirabell and Millamant a model of two people possessed of an appreciation of what a knowledge of poetry, art, and the drama may provide in the way of understanding the world. It is, after all, they, not Fainall, who triumph. I would add to this now not only the love and sincerity that move both of them but also the larger lesson provided by the story of Mrs. Fainall and the "moral" pointing to her example.

Would anyone in the original audience of 1700 have understood anything like such a basic fable behind *The Way of the World*? That they would have seen through Congreve's private war with Collier and even the outline of his fable seems extremely doubtful. How could anyone delighted by Lady Wishfort's attempting, with the help of her maid Foible, to repair the "old peel'd Wall" (2:154 [III.v, 72]) that is her face, or by the proviso scene between Mirabell and Millamant pay attention to a larger political moral. That does not mean that the anger that Congreve nursed against Collier for forcing him into a critical battle on a level that he considered to be beneath his intelligence was not genuine. He even laments that he was ever attracted to writing for the stage: "And I through the remainder of my Indiscretion, suffer'd my self to be drawn in, to the prosecution of a difficult and thankless Study; and to be involved in a perpetual War with Knaves and Fools" (3:90–91 [ll. 583–86]).

We know of Congreve's later portrait of himself as a "contemplative" and the association with the philosophy of George Berkeley on matters of time and ideas.[37] To this interest may be added the suggestion of Lockean psychology that appears in his *The Mourning Bride*.[38] Such a view is more than supported by his explanation of the way humans absorb experience that appears in his *Amendments of Mr. Collier's False and Imperfect Citations*. Criticizing Collier's imagery, Congreve writes,

> Pitiful and mean Comparisons, proceed from pitiful and mean *Ideas*: and such *Ideas* have their beginning from a familiarity with such Objects. From this Author's poor and filthy Metaphors and Similitudes, we may learn the Filthiness of his Imagination; and from the Uncleanness of that, we may make a reasonable guess at his rate of Education, and those Objects with which he has been most conversant and familiar. (3:114 [ll. 1452–59])

Congreve's snobbery aside, he tries to lesson Collier on matters of language, perception, and response. And to later readers of *The Way of the World* he left a complex pattern of meanings, including a vision of the world that was, in the broadest sense, political.

Notes

1. Thomas Heyrick, *Miscellany Poems* (Cambridge, 1691), iv.
2. Congreve was later to complain about her acting. See *William Congreve: Letters & Documents*, ed. John Hodges (New York: Harcourt, Brace, & World, 1964), 21–22.
3. William Congreve, *The Works of William Congreve*, ed. D. F. McKenzie and C. Y. Ferdinand, 3 vols. (Oxford: Oxford University Press, 2011), 2:223 [V.xiv. ll. 48–51]. Citations from *The Way of the World* and other works by Congreve will be referred to this edition and placed within parentheses in my text.
4. They state further that Mirabell is not "an idealized character [...] But he is by the standards of the world of the play an honourable man" (1:565). Milhous and Hume do not clarify the basis for their ethical judgments.
5. Julia Stone Peters, *Congreve, the Drama and the Printed Word* (Stanford, CA: Stanford University Press, 1990), 24–25.
6. Richard Braverman, "Capital Relations and the Way of the World," *English Literary History* 52 (Spring 1988): 133–44.
7. Scott Mackenzie, "Sexual Arithmetic: Appetite and Consumption in *The Way of the World*," *Eighteenth-Century Studies* 47 (2014): 261–76.
8. In *Der englische Frauenroman und andere Aufsätze, Schweizer Anglistische Arbeiten*, 88 (Bern: A. Francke AG Verlag, 1976): 164–75.
9. As I will attempt to demonstrate, Congreve has his own vision of the Restoration up to the Glorious Revolution as a struggle against despotism and puritan morality. But he seems to have believed that the triumph of William and Mary had firmly established a degree of political and moral tolerance in Britain. The contempt with which he treated Jeremy Collier, who, in Congreve's mind, represented both an antiquated Puritanism and Jacobitism, suggests that the popularity of Collier's attitude toward the stage and the national flirtation with Jacobitism, leading to the Jacobite invasion of 1715, probably came as a surprise to him.
10. Although Filmer's *Patriarcha* created a stir when it was published in 1680, most scholars agree that it was written mainly in the 1620s. It was a weapon in the hands of the Tory opponents of the Whig supporters of the exclusion of the Duke of York, later James II, from the throne. But, as H. T. Dickinson argued, "The Glorious Revolution of 1688 delivered a severe blow to the extreme Tory position" on a variety of doctrines, including the patriarchal claim to the throne. *Liberty and Property* (New York: Holmes and Meier, 1977), 27, 33–39. See also J. G. A Pocock, *The Ancient Constitution and the Feudal Law* (New York: Norton, 1967), 231; and Steve Pincus, *1688: The First Modern Revolution* (New Haven, CT: Yale, 2009), 294–96. For the continued use of patriarchal theory after 1688, especially among those who refused to accept the tenets of the Glorious Revolution, such as the Jacobites, see Gordon Schochet, *Patriarchalism in Political Thought* (New York: Basic Books, 1975), 209–24. As a Whig and a loyal supporter of the monarchy, Congreve had no need to read the printed work of Locke or Algernon Sidney in manuscript to know that William and Mary had better claims as "conquerors" than by patriarchal right.

11   Although the Act of Settlement did not pass until 1701, William III had been active during 1699 in getting the succession given to the person who became George I after the death of Queen Anne. The Act of Settlement gave Parliament the right to choose the successor to the throne. See Stephen Baxter, *William III and the Defense of European Liberty* (New York: Harcourt, Brace & World, 1966), 371–72.
12   For a discussion of the bad effects of this action upon the Protestant community in Ireland, see *Short Remarks upon the Late Act of Resumption of the Irish Forfeitures* (1701), in John Somers, *A Collection of Scarce and Valuable Tracts ... Particularly That of the Late Lord Somers*, ed. Walter Scott, 13 vols. (London: T. Cadell, 1814), 11:228–36.
13   Baxter, *William III*, 370.
14   *Cursory Remarks* (London, 1699); and *A Just Rebuke* (London, 1699).
15   Richard Newman, *The Complaint of English Subjects* (London, 1699), sig. A3, 20.
16   In the introduction to his *Intrigues at Versailles, or, A Jilt in all Humours*(London, 1697), D'Urfey describes how Congreve and Betterton sat together to hear the play.
17   See the accounts in Lawrence Stone, *The Road to Divorce* (Oxford: Oxford University Press, 1990), 317–22. Although the first fifty years of the eighteenth century saw almost no divorces, in the 1690s, with the cases of the Earl of Macclesfield, Lord Norfolk, and Ralph Box, it must have seemed as if divorces might become relatively common. In addition, both the Macclesfield and Norfolk cases involved the wife's demand that she have her portion returned to her as part of the divorce.
18   Mrs. Fainall is not present when Marwood delivers her vivid image of what a court scene for a divorce might look like, but Marwood's account is intended for Lady Wishfort—her concern for reputation and sense of embarrassment.
19   Anthony Ashley Cooper, 3rd Earl of Shaftesbury, *Characteristicks of Men, Manners, Opinions, Times*, ed. Philip Ayers. 2 vols. (Oxford: Clarendon Press, 1999).
20   See Peter Laslett, "Introduction," in John Locke, *Two Treatises of Government* (Cambridge: Cambridge University Press, 1967), 112–20.
21   See Richard Kroll, *Restoration Drama and the "Circle of Commerce"* (Cambridge: Cambridge University Press, 2007), 283–91.
22   See Shirley Strum Kenny, ed., *Plays*, by Richard Steele (Oxford: Clarendon Press, 1971), 275.
23   In Southerne's *The Wive's Excuse* (1692), the Friendlys, an ill-matched couple, agree at the end to go their separate ways. And the subtitle, *Cuckold's Make Themselves*, points to Mr. Friendly as a fool who places an impossible burden on his wife.
24   He was made one of five commissioners for licensing hackney coaches in 1695 and commissioner for wines after that. See John Hodges, *Congreve* (New York: Modern Language Association, 1941), 84.
25   See Jean Claude Helvetius, *De L'Esprit: Or, Essays on the Mind, and Its Several Faculties* (London, 1759), 37.
26   William Congreve, *The Library of William Congreve*, ed. John Hodges (New York: New York Public Library, 1955), 61.
27   René Le Bossu, *Monsieur Bossu's Treatise of the Epick Poem* (London, 1695), 22–23.
28   Ibid., 17.
29   George Farquhar, *Works*, ed. Charles Stonehill, 2 vols. (London: Nonesuch, 1930), 2:336.
30   Ibid.. It should be noted that Congreve translated, or rather "imitated" two poetic fables of Jean de la Fontaine, "An Impossible Thing" and "The Peasant in Search of His Heifer."

31 For two excellent studies of the beast fable at this time, see Annabel Patterson, *Fables of Power* (Durham, NC: Duke University Press, 1989); and Jayne Lewis, *The English Fable* (Cambridge: Cambridge University Press, 1996). In 1695–96, Vanbrugh adapted a French comedy on Aesop as a courtier, in which despite the insults to which he is subjected about his deformed appearance, he delivers wise suggestions through his fables.

32 Although Mrs. Fainall is happy to learn that she has *evidence* of her husband's adultery provided by the servants, Mincing and Foible, she hardly seems surprised by the fact itself. Nothing in the text of the play allows the audience to be certain that Mrs. Fainall knows of her husband's affair, but she recognizes Marwood as a sexual predator from the beginning of the play and is antagonistic toward her throughout. Similarly in the first scene of the play, Mirabell, Mrs. Fainall's intimate friend, reveals an awareness of Fainall's relationship with Marwood.

33 See, e.g., James Wright, *Historia Histrionica: An Historical Account of the English Stage* (London, 1699), 32.

34 See Dennis's *The Usefulness of the Stage*, in *Critical Works*, ed. E. N. Hooker, 2 vols. (Baltimore, MD: Johns Hopkins University Press, 1939–43), 1:168.

35 Collier's *Short View*, with its complaint about the mockery addressed toward the clergy, would have made it impossible to cast Fainall as a clergyman, but in Congreve's mind casting his hypocritical villain as a libertine might not have seemed so completely at odds with the character of a clergyman. In his reply to Collier, he compared Collier's attacks to "a sinful Pedagogue" who "sometimes lashes a pretty Boy, that looks lovely in his Eyes, for Reasons best known to himself" (3:112). In much the same way, Fainall reveals a sadistic streak from the very beginning when he boasts of his lack of pleasure in gambling with someone who did not care about losing or having an affair with a woman who was unconcerned about her reputation. See the *Amendments of Collier's False and Imperfect Citations*. Congreve also states that Collier displayed a *"Libertine Stroke"* (3:76) in his writing.

36 For the impossibility of Congreve's task, see Maximillian Novak, "The Artist and the Clergyman," *College English* 30 (1969): 555–61.

37 D. F. Mackenzie, "Richard Van Bleeck's Painting of William Congreve as Contemplative (1715)," *Review of English Studies* 51 (2000): 41–61. D. F. McKenzie attempted to analyze the implications of having a volume of Berkeley's philosophic writings among the books with which Congreve is portrayed.

38 D. F. McKenzie and C. Y. Ferdinand rightly annotate two speeches in *The Mourning Bride* by referring to John Locke's *Essay Concerning Human Understanding*. See Congreve, *Works*, 2:551–52. For a contemporary criticism of Congreve for demanding that his reader be a "Philosopher," see *The Town Display'd, in a Letter to Amintor in the Country* (London, 1701).

AFTERWORD

I began by remarking on the notion that no important critic or historian has suggested that the period of time spanning the end of the seventeenth century and the beginning of the eighteenth centuries might be called the "Age of Congreve." This is hardly surprising. This is a period dominated by John Locke in philosophy and Isaac Newton in the sciences. In literary studies, writers such as John Dryden, Daniel Defoe, Jonathan Swift, Joseph Addison, and Alexander Pope were in many ways more formidable. Congreve was essentially a dramatist, and a dramatist who had the misfortune to have been writing at a time that was notably condemned for its immorality by the critics of the periods that followed. The authors of the *Tatler* and *Spectator*, Sir Richard Steele and Joseph Addison, those arbiters of taste for the early eighteenth century, demonstrated the ethical unworthiness of the comedies of the previous fifty years, and while they spared Congreve, his works were clearly implicated.[1] Later in the century, although Samuel Johnson's condemnation was intended mainly for the writers of the period of Charles II, his remarks in his "Prologue … Opening of the Theatre in Drury Lane 1747" would have been aimed at Congreve and his contemporaries as well:

> Themselves they studied, as they felt, they writ,
> Intrigue was Plot, Obscenity was Wit.
> Vice always found a sympathetick Friend;
> They pleas'd their Age, and did not aim to mend.

Once "Shame" and "Virtue" triumphed over the immorality of the period, the playwrights of this period could not find an audience, though they "proudly hop'd to pimp in future Days."[2] In order to fully recover from what essentially a period of censorship in English drama, Congreve would have had to have been an even stronger, and more popular, writer than he was. Oscar Wilde brought witty comedy back to the English stage in the 1890s, but to some extent many producers have probably felt that audiences might prefer a slightly dated Wilde to an inevitably more dated Congreve.

If, then, Congreve has struggled somewhat on the stage, how has he done on the page, to use the usual dichotomy? Here again, Congreve has not done as well as might be expected. Although *The Way of the World* had been a standard text in surveys of British literature, such as the *Norton Anthology of English Literature*, more recently it has occasionally been replaced by Aphra Behn's *The Rover* or even Thomas Southerne's theatrical version of Behn's "novel," *Oroonoko*, as large anthologies have yielded to individually chosen texts. The period anthology edited by Geoffrey Tillotson, Paul Fussell, Jr., and Marshall Waingrow preferred John Dryden's *Marriage A-la Mode* as a representative Restoration comedy, a choice that might be easily defended on the basis of its unique playfulness and wit.

Still, there is a defense to be made for Congreve. Jonathan Swift found himself staying up all night in reading through a volume of Congreve's plays, finding the comedy irresistible. In this volume, I have not emphasized how funny Congreve could be. I think that is a given. The confrontation between Foresight and Sir Sampson Legend in *Love for Love* has to be one of the great moments in comic literature, and Lady Wishfort's delusions about her possible attractiveness to her imaginary suitors make her into an unforgettable, archetypal figure in world literature.

I have not attempted to make this defense. Instead, I have tried to provide a series of supplementary readings under the umbrella of "politics." In some instances, I have entered into the politics of the period to show how deeply his plays drew upon contemporary disputes and conflicts. At other times, I have attempted to examine the epistemological milieu that swirled about the 1690s as thickly as the intrigues between the supporters of the deposed monarch, James II, and the defenders of the new monarchs, William (later William III) and Mary. In addition to the inescapable political and philosophic turmoil of these times, it was also a period of immense social and economic change and unrest. That the material of these changes should have gotten into Congreve's plays is hardly surprising. I have tried to argue for what amounts to a complex pattern of meanings within these plays. I am not arguing that Congreve functioned as a political philosopher within his plays, but it may certainly be said that he expected his audience, both in the theater and his readers, to be aware of the potential political meanings behind his plots and characters.

Notes

1   Both *Love for Love* and *The Old Batchelor* are praised in *The Spectator*.
2   Samuel Johnson, *Poems*, ed. David Nichol Smith and Edward McAdam (Oxford: Clarendon University Press, 1962), 51–53. For a discussion of Johnson's attitude toward the Restoration, see my "Johnson and the Wild Vicissitudes of Taste," in *The Unknown Samuel Johnson*, ed. John Burke and Donald Kay (Madison: University of Wisconsin Press, 1983), 54–75.

WORKS CITED

Abbadie, Jacques. *The History of the Late Conspiracy against the King and the Nation.* London, 1696.
Abercromby, David. *A Moral Discourse of the Power of Interest.* London, 1690.
Alleman, Gellert. *Matrimonial Law in Restoration Comedy.* Philadelphia, PA: Wallingford, 1942.
An Answer to Mr. Collier's Defence. London, 1696.
Antiquity Reviv'd: Or, the Government of a Certain Island Anciently Call'd Astreada. London, 1693.
Ashcraft, Richard, and Alan Roper. *Politics as Reflected in Literature.* Los Angeles: William Andrews Clark Memorial Library, 1989.
Astell, Mary. *A Farther Essay Relating to the Female-Sex.* London, 1696.
Bahlman, Dudley. *The Moral Revolution of 1688.* New Haven, CT: Yale University Press, 1957.
Bailey, Nathaniel. *Dictionarium Britannicum.* London, 1730.
Barbon, Nicholas. *A Discourse of Trade.* London, 1690.
Barish, Jonas. *The Antitheatrical Prejudice.* Berkeley: University of California Press, 1981.
Barton, Samuel. *A Sermon Preached before the King and Queen at Whitehall, the 27th of October. For Victory at Sea.* London, 1692.
Bateson, F. W., ed. *The Works of William Congreve.* London: Peter Davies, 1930.
Baxter, Stephen. *William III and the Defense of European Liberty.* New York: Harcourt, Brace & World, 1966.
Bedford, Arthur. *The Evil and Danger of Stage Plays.* London, 1706.
Borges, Jorge Luis. *Labyrinths.* Edited by Donald Yates and James Irby. New York: New Directions, 1964.
Boswell, James. *Life of Johnson,* 2 vols. New York: Oxford University Press, 1948.
Braverman, Richard. "Capital Relations and the Way of the World." *English Literary History,* 52. Baltimore, MD: English Literary History, 1988.
———. *Plots and Counterplots.* Cambridge: Cambridge University Press, 1993.
Bullokar, John Bullokar. *An English Expositour.* Cambridge, 1676.
Burgis, S. *Wit for Money: Or, Poet Stutter.* London, 1692.
Burthogge, Richard. *An Essay upon Reason and the Nature of Spirits.* London, 1694.
Cameron, William. *Poems on Affairs of State.* New Haven, CT: Yale University Press, 1963–75.
Canfield, J. Douglas. *Nicholas Rowe and Christian Tragedy.* Gainesville: University of Florida Press, 1957.
Childs, John. *The Nine Years' War and the British Army, 1688–1697: The Operations in the Low Countries.* Manchester: Manchester University Press, 1991.
Collier, Jeremy. *Defence of His Absolution of Sir William Parkins, at the Place of Execution.* London: 1696.
———. *A Short View of the Immorality and Profaneness of the English Stage.* Introduction by Yugi Kankeko. London: Routledge/Thoemmes Press, 1996.

Congreve, William. *Amendments of Collier's False and Imperfect Citations.* London, 1698.
———. *The Library of William Congreve.* Edited by John Hodges. New York: New York Public Library, 1955.
———. *William Congreve: The Critical Heritage.* Edited by Alexander Lindsay and Howard Erskine-Hill. London: Routledge, 1989.
———. *William Congreve: Letters & Documents.* Edited by John Hodges. New York: Harcourt, Brace, & World, 1964.
———. *The Works of William Congreve.* Edited by D. F. McKenzie and C. Y. Ferdinand, 3 vols. Oxford: Oxford University Press, 2011.
Cooper, Anthony Ashley. *Characteristicks of Men, Manners, Opinions, Times.* Edited by Philip Ayers, 2 vols. Oxford: Clarendon Press, 1999.
Crowne, John. *The English Friar.* London, 1690.
———. *The Married Beau: Or, the Curious Impertinent,* in *Dramatic Works.* Edited by James Maidment and W. H. Logan, 5 vols. Edinburgh: W. Patterson, 1874.
Cursory Remarks. London, 1699.
David, Madeline V. *Le débat sur les écritures et l' hiéroglyphe aux xviie et xviiie siècles.* Paris: S.E.V.P.E.N., 1965.
Davies, Thomas. *Life of Garrick,* 2 vols. London, 1780.
Declaration of the Sense of the Archbishops and Bishops Now in and about London. London, 1696.
Defoe, Daniel. *An Essay upon Projects.* Edited by Joyce Kennedy, Michael Seidel, and Maximillian E. Novak. New York: AMS Press, 1999.
Dennis, John. *The Usefulness of the Stage,* in *Critical Works.* Edited by E. N. Hooker, 2 vols. Baltimore, MD: Johns Hopkins University Press, 1939–43.
Derrida, Jacques. *Of Grammatology.* Translated by Gayatri Spivak. Baltimore, MD: Johns Hopkins University Press, 1976.
Dickinson, H. T. *Liberty and Property.* New York: Holmes and Meier, 1977.
Dieckmann, Liselotte. *Hieroglyphics.* St. Louis, MO: Washington University Press, 1970.
Dilke, Thomas. *The Lover's Luck.* London, 1696.
Dr. Sherlock Vindicated, or Cogent Reasons Why That Worthy Person Hath Complied with the Necessity of the Times, and Why He at First Refused It. London, 1691.
Dryden, J., A. Marvell, T. Sprat, and E. Waller. *A Collection of the Newest and Most Ingenious Poems, Songs, Catches, etc. against Popery.* London, 1689.
Dryden, John. *Discourse Concerning the Original and Progress of Satire,* in *Of Dramatic Poesy and Other Critical Essays.* Edited by George Watson. London: Dent, 1962.
———. *Letters.* Edited by Charles Wald. New York: AMS Press, 1965.
———. *Works.* Edited by H. T. Swedenberg et al., 20 vols. Berkeley: University of California Press, 1956–2000.
Dunton, John. *Athenian Mercury.* London: Athenian Society, 1691.
D'Urfey, Thomas. *The Banditti.* London, 1686.
———. *The Intrigues of Versailles: A Jilt in All Humours.* London, 1697.
———. *Love for Money: Or, the Boarding School.* London, 1691.
———. *The Marriage Hater Match'd.* London, 1692.
———. *The Moralists.* London, 1691.
———. *The Richmond Heiress.* London, 1693.
———. *The Weesils.* London, 1691.
Estienne, Henri. *The Art of Making Devises: Treating of Hieroglyphics, Symboles, Emblemes, … Reverses of Medals.* Translated by Thomas Blount. London, 1650.
Farquhar, George. *The Complete Works,* ed. Charles Stonehill, 2 vols. London: Nonesuch, 1930.

Filmer, Edward. *A Defence of Plays: Or the Stage Vindicated, from Several Passages in Mr. Collier's Short View.* London: 1707.
Filmer, Robert. *Patriarcha and Other Writings.* Edited by Johan Sommerville. Cambridge: Cambridge University Press, 1991.
Fujimura, Thomas. *The Restoration Comedy of Wit.* Princeton, NJ: Princeton University Press, 1952.
Gould, Robert. *The Folly of Love: A New Satyr against Women,* 2nd ed. London, 1693.
———. *The Works of Robert Gould.* London, 1709.
Gracián, Baltasar. *The Courtier's Manual: Or, the Art of Prudence.* Translated by John Savage. London, 1685.
———. *A Truth-Telling Manual and the Art of Worldly Wisdom,* 2nd ed. Translated by Martin Fischer. Springfield, IL: Charles Thomas Press, 1945.
Hamou, Philippe. "Locke and Descartes on Selves and Thinking Substances," in *Locke and Cartesian Philosophy,* ed. Philippe Hamour and Martine Pécharman. Oxford: Oxford University Press, 2018.
Harth, Philip. *Pen for a Party: Dryden's Tory Propaganda in Its Contexts.* Princeton, NJ: Princeton University Press, 1993.
Hawkins, Harriet. *Likenesses of Truth in Elizabethan and Restoration Drama.* Oxford: Clarendon Press, 1972.
Helvetius, Jean Claude. *De L'Esprit: Or, Essays on the Mind, and Its Several Faculties.* London, 1759.
Heyrick, Thomas. *Miscellany Poems.* Cambridge, 1691.
Hobbes, Thomas. *Leviathan.* Introduction by C. B. Macpherson. London: Penguin, 1985.
Hodges, John. *Congreve the Man.* New York: Modern Language Association, 1941.
Hody, Humphrey. *Animadversions on Two Pamphlets Lately Published.* London, 1696.
Holland, Norman. *The First Modern Comedies.* Cambridge: Harvard University Press, 1959.
Hughes, Derek. "The 'Example Theory' and the Providentialist Approach to Restoration Drama: Some Questions of Validity and Applicability," *The Eighteenth Century: Theory and Interpretation* 24 (1983): 103–14.
Hume, Robert. *The Development of English Drama in the Late Seventeenth Century.* Oxford: Clarendon Press, 1976.
———. "The myth of the Rake in Restoration Comedy," *Studies in the Literary Imagination* (Issue 24). Georgia: Georgia State University Press, 1983.
Inchbald, Elizabeth. *Remarks for the British Theatre, 1806–1809.* Introduction by Cecilia Macheski. Delmar, NY: Scholars Facsimiles, 1990.
Irving, H. B. *The Life of Judge Jeffreys.* London: William Heinemann, 1898.
Jeffries, George. *The Arraignment and Tryal of the Late Reverend Mr. Thomas Rosewell, for High-Treason; before the Lord Chief Jefferies.* London, 1715.
Johnson, Samuel. *An Argument Proving That the Abrogation of King James by the people of England from the Regal Throne and Promotion of the Prince of Orange ... to the Throne of England in His Stead, Was According to the Constitution of the English Government.* London, 1692.
Johnson, Samuel (Dr.). *Lives of the English Poets.* Introduction by Arthur Waugh, 2 vols. London: Oxford University Press, 1972.
———. *Poems.* Edited by David Nichol Smith and Edward McAdam. Oxford: Clarendon University Press, 1962.
Jurieu, Pierre. *Monsieur Jurieu's Judgment upon the Question of Defending our Religion by Arms.* London, 1689.
———. *A Just Rebuke.* London, 1699.
Kinservik, Matthew. *Disciplining Satire: The Censorship of Satiric Comedy on the*

Eighteenth-Century London Stage. Lewisburg: Bucknell University Press, 2002.

Kircher, Athanasius. *Oedipus Aegyptiacus*. Rome, 1652.

Kroll, Richard Kroll. *Restoration Drama and the "Circle of Commerce"*. Cambridge: Cambridge University Press, 2007.

Lamb, Charles. *Complete Works and Letters of Charles Lamb*. Introduction by Saxe Commins. New York: Modern Library, 1935.

———. "On the Artificial Comedy of the Last Century," in *The Works of Charles and Mary Lamb*, ed. E. V. Lucas. London: Methuen, 1912.

Le Bossu, René. *Monsieur Bossu's Treatise of the Epick Poem*. London, 1695.

Lévi-Strauss, Claude. *The Savage Mind*. London: Weidenfeld and Nicolson, 1962.

Lewis, Jayne. *The English Fable*. Cambridge: Cambridge University Press, 1996.

Lindsay, Alexander, and Howard Erskine Hill, eds. See under *Congreve: The Critical Heritage*.

Locke, John. *An Essay Concerning Human Understanding*. Edited by Alexander Fraser, 2 vols. Oxford: Oxford University Press, 1891; reprint Dover Press, 1959.

———. *Two Treatises*. Edited Peter Laslet. Cambridge: Cambridge University Press, 1960.

Luttrell, Narcissus. *A Brief Relation of State Affairs*. Oxford, 1857.

Mackenzie, D. F. "Richard Van Bleeck's Painting of William Congreve as Contemplative (1715)," *Review of English Studies* 51 (2000): 41–61.

Mackenzie, Scott. "Sexual Arithmetic: Appetite and Consumption in *The Way of the World*," *Eighteenth-Century Studies* 47 (2014): 261–74.

Mandeville, Bernard. *The Fable of the Bees*. Edited by F. B. Kaye, 2 vols. Oxford: Clarendon Press, 1957.

Markley, Robert. "Hariett Hawkins and the Criticism of the 1970s," in *Style*. Newark, NJ: Delaware University Press, 2005.

Memoires Concerning the Campagne of Three Kings, William, Lewis, and James in the Year 1692. London, 1693.

Menestrier, François. *La Philosophie des images énigmatique*. Lyon, 1694.

Meriton, L. *Pecuniae Obediunt Omnia: Money Does Master All Things*. London, 1696.

Montgomery, James. *Great Britain's Just Complaint for Her Late Measures, Present Sufferings, Future Miseries She Is Exposed to*. London, 1691.

Modest Enquiry into the Causes of the Present Disasters in England. London, 1690.

Motteux, Peter. *Love's a Jest*. Buck, 1696.

Mountfort, William. *Greenwich-Park*. London, 1691.

Mullet, Charles Mullet. "A Case of Allegiance: William Sherlock and the Revolution of 1688," *Huntington Library Quarterly* 10 (1946): 83–103.

Newman, Richard. *The Complaint of English Subjects*. London, 1699.

Novak, Maximillian E. "The Artist and the Clergyman," *College English* (Issue 30). Urbana, IL: National Council of Teachers of English, 1969.

———. *Congreve*. New York: Twayne, 1970.

———. "Congreve as the Eighteenth Century Archetypal Libertine," *Restoration and Eighteenth Century Theatre Research* (Issue 15). Carbondale: Southern Illinois University Press, 1976.

———. "Criticism and the Discourses of History in the Restoration and Eighteenth Century," in *Theory and Tradition in Eighteenth-Century Studies*, ed. Richard Schwarz, 104–17. Carbondale: Southern Illinois University Press, 1990.

———. "Johnson and the Wild Vicissitudes of Taste," in *The Unknown Samuel Johnson*, ed. John Burke and Donald Kay. Madison: University of Wisconsin Press, 1983.

Nussbaum, Felicity. "The Unaccountable Pleasure of Eighteenth-Century Tragedy," *Publications of the Modern Language Association* 129 (2014): 688–707.
Ogg, David. *England in the Reigns of James II and William III.* Oxford, Clarendon Press, 1966.
Owen, Susan. *Restoration Theatre and Crisis.* Oxford: Clarendon Press, 1996.
Patterson, Annabel. *Fables of Power.* Durham, NC: Duke University Press, 1989.
Peters, Julia Stone. *Congreve, the Drama, and the Printed Word.* Stanford, CA: Stanford University Press, 1991.
Phillips, John. *Reflection on Our Modern Poesy.* London: 1695.
Pincus, Steve. *1688: The First Modern Revolution.* New Haven, CT: Yale University Press, 2009.
Pocock, J. G. A. *The Ancient Constitution and the Feudal Law.* New York: Norton, 1967.
Powell, George. *A Very Good Wife.* London, 1693.
Prager, Jeffrey. *Presenting the Past: Psychoanalysis and the Sociology of Misremembering.* Cambridge: Harvard University Press, 1998.
Prynne, William. *Historic-Mastix.* London, 1633.
Pufendorf, Samuel. *Law of Nature.* London, 1703.
Racine, Jean. *Athalie,* in *Théatre Complet,* ed. Maurice Rat. Paris: Garnier Frères, 1953.
Richardson, Mr., *Providence and Precept: Or, the Case of Doing Evil That Good May Come of It.* London, 1691.
Ridpath, George. *The Stage Acquitted. Being a Full Answer to Mr. Collier, and the Other Enemies of the Drama.* London, 1699.
Robb, Nisca. *William of Orange,* 2 vols. London: Heinemann, 1966.
Rymer, Thomas. *Critical Writings.* Edited by Curt Zimansky. New Haven, CT: Yale University Press, 1956.
Saint-Evremond, Charles de. *Works.* London, 1700.
Schneider, Ben Ross. *The Ethos of Restoration Comedy.* Urbana: University of Illinois University Press, 1971.
Schochet, Gordon Schochet. *Patriarchalism in Political Thought.* New York: Basic Books, 1975.
Scouten, Arthur, et al., ed. *The London Stage*, 11 vols. Carbondale: Southern Illinois University Press, 1960–68.
Shadwell, Thomas. *The Volunteers.* London: Fortune Press, 1927.
Shakespeare, William. *Romeo and Juliet.* Edited by Brian Gibbons. London: Methuen, 1980.
Sherlock, William. *A Discourse Concerning the Divine Providence,* 3rd ed. London: William Rogers, 1702.
Somers, John. *Collection of Scarce and Valuable Tracts ... Particularly That of the Late Lord Somers.* Edited by Walter Scott, 13 vols. London: T. Cadell, 1814.
Spence, Joseph. *Anecdotes, Observations, and Characters of Books and Men.* Edited by James Osborn. Oxford: Clarendon Press, 1966.
The Stage Acquitted. London, 1699.
The State of Parties, and of the Publick. London, 1692.
Staves, Susan. *Married Women's Separate Property in England, 1660–1833.* Cambridge: Harvard University Press, 1990.
Steele, Richard. *The Plays of Sir Richard Steele.* Edited by Shirley Strum Kenny. Oxford: Clarendon Press, 1971.
Stone, Lawrence. *The Road to Divorce.* Oxford: Oxford University Press, 1990.
Strawson, Galen. *Locke on Personal Identity: Consciousness and Concernment.* Princeton, NJ: Princeton University Press, 2011.

Swedenberg, H. T., ed. *Congreve Consider'd*. Los Angeles: William Andrews Clark Memorial Library, 1971.
Taylor, D. Crane. *William Congreve*. New York: Russell & Russell, 1963.
The Town Display'd in a Letter to Amintor in the Country. London, 1701.
Trimming Court Divine. London, 1690.
Underwood, Dale. *Etherege and the Seventeenth-Century Comedy of Manners*. Yale Studies in English 135. New Haven, CT: Yale University Press, 1957.
Van Lennep, William, ed. *The London Stage 1660–1800: A Calendar of Plays, Entertainments & Afterpieces together with Casts, Box-Receipts and Contemporary Comment*. Carbondale: Southern Illinois University Press, 1960–68.
Vanbrugh, John. *Complete Works*. Edited by Bonamy Dobrée and Geoffrey Webb, 4 vols. London: Nonesuch, 1927.
Velissariou, Aspasia. "The Vicissitudes of Resemblance in Congreve's *Incognita*," *Journal of the Short Story* (Issue 39). Nashville, TN: Belmont University Press, 2002.
Walsh, William. *A Dialogue Concerning Women, Being a Defence of the Sex*. London, 1691.
Warburton, William. *The Divine Legation of Moses Demonstrated*. London: Thomas Tegg, 1837.
Ward, Ned. *The Miracles Perform'd by Money*. London, 1692.
Watt, Ian. *The Rise of the Novel*. Berkeley: University of California Press, 1959.
Weber, Harold. *The Restoration Rake-Hero*. Madison: University of Wisconsin Press, 1986.
Wildi, Max. "Locke's Conception of the Conjugal Contract and Congreve's Proviso Scene in *The Way of the World*." *Der englische Frauenroman und andere Aufsätze, Schweizer Anglistische Arbeiten* (Issue 88). Bern: A. Francke AG Verlag, 1976.
Williams, Aubrey. *An Approach to Congreve*. New Haven, CT: Yale University Press, 1979.
Winn, James Anderson. *John Dryden and His World*. New Haven, CT: Yale University Press, 1987.
Wright, James. *Historia Histrionica: An Historical Account of the English Stage*. London, 1699.
———. *The Humours, and Conversations of the Town*. London, 1693.
Wright, Thomas. *The Female Vertuoso*. London, 1693.
Wycherley, William. *The Country Wife*. London, 1676.
Zimbardo, Rose. *Wycherley's Drama*. Yale Studies in English 156. New Haven, CT: Yale University Press, 1959.

INDEX

Abbadie, Jacques 97, 100
Abercromby, David 48
Alleman, Gellert 13
Ashcraft, Richard 46
Astell, Mary 12, 14

Bailey, Nathaniel 84
Bahlman, Dudley 5, 6, 13
Barbon, Nicholas 40, 41, 48
Barish, Jonas 33, 45
Barry, Elizabeth 86, 101
Barton, Samuel 56, 64
Baxter, Stephen 63, 64, 99, 104, 118
Bedford, Arthur 9, 13
Betterton, Thomas 17, 101, 102, 104, 118
Borges, Jorge Luis 40, 48
Boswell, James 92, 93, 99
Bracegirdle, Anne 101, 108
Braverman, Richard 33, 45, 47, 103, 105, 117
Bullokar, John Bullokar 84
Burthogge, Richard 7, 99, 100

Cameron, William 64
Canfield, J. Douglas 58, 64
Charles II 6, 34, 35, 40, 46, 113, 121
Childs, John 48
Collier, Jeremy 6, 9, 17, 18, 21, 23, 24, 25, 31, 33, 44, 51, 56, 58, 59, 62, 63, 64, 87, 97, 99, 100, 104, 105, 110, 111, 113, 114, 115, 116, 117, 119
Congreve, William, Reputation, milieu, and politics xi, xii, 1–14, 16–21, 22–76, 79–84, 86–92, 93–105, 107–19
  Amendments of Mr. Colliers...Citations 104, 110, 111, 112, 116, 119

The Double Dealer 1, 3, 4, 33, 51–66, 80, 102, 105, 106, 109, 110, 111, 115;
Incognita 17, 18, 26–31, 45, 90
Love for Love 6, 19, 22, 33, 66–87, 103, 111, 122
The Mourning Bride 18, 22, 26, 31, 33, 47, 87–99, 116, 119
The Old Batchelor 25, 34–50, 62, 108, 112, 122
The Way of the World 2, 25, 33, 81, 97, 101–20
Cooper, Anthony Ashley, 3rd earl of Shaftesbury 107, 118
Crowne, John 12, 14, 17, 104

David, Madeline V. 83
Davies, Thomas 22, 24, 25, 30
Defoe, Daniel 1, 48, 55, 81, 104, 121
Dennis, John 114, 119
Derrida, Jacques 84
Dickinson, H. T. 117
Dieckmann, Liselotte 83
Dilke, Thomas 13, 104
Divorce 3, 81, 105, 106, 118
D'Urfey, Thomas 4, 5, 7, 13, 14, 30, 34, 44, 45, 46, 48, 49, 54, 68, 81, 84, 104, 118
Dryden, John 1, 4, 5, 7, 13, 17, 34, 36, 39, 40, 45, 46, 47, 51, 56, 57, 63, 68, 89, 99, 100, 121, 122
Dunton, John 106

epistemology 2, 7, 17, 19, 21, 23, 25, 26, 27, 29, 31, 91
Erskine Hill, Howard 31, 47, 99
Estienne, Henry 83

experience 6, 10, 19, 27, 28, 29, 33, 34, 39, 69, 71, 72, 75, 87, 91, 92, 94, 96, 98, 100, 112, 116

fable 30, 41, 69, 101–19
Farquhar, John 5, 112, 118
Filmer, Edward 31
Filmer, Robert 68, 83, 103, 117
Fujimura, Thomas 57, 64

Gould, Robert 13, 14, 41, 47, 48
Gracián, Baltasar 11, 107

Hamou, Philippe 31
Harth, Philip 34, 46
Hawkins, Harriet 58, 64, 99
Helvetius, Jean Claude 110, 118
Heyrick, Thomas 117
hieroglyphics 69–84
Hobbes, Thomas 2, 67, 83
Hodges, John 38, 47, 117, 118
Hody, Humphrey 100
Holland, Norman 57, 64
Hughes, Derek 58, 64
Hume, Robert 17, 58, 64, 102, 117

identity 19, 26, 27–31, 90
Inchbald, Elizabeth 99
Irving, H. B. 46

Jacobitism 105, 111, 117
James II xi, xii, 6, 13, 17, 30, 34, 36, 37, 38, 39, 40, 42, 43, 46, 47, 53, 55, 63, 81, 88, 89, 96, 104, 111, 113, 114, 122
Jeffries, George 46
Johnson, Samuel 23, 24, 31, 56, 64, 92, 93, 121
Jurieu, Pierre 61, 88, 99

Kinservik, Matthew 31
Kircher, Athanasius 69, 81, 83
Kroll, Richard Kroll 108, 118

Lamb, Charles 2, 5, 13, 33, 45, 57
language; of sensibility 95
Le Bossu, René 110, 118
Leigh, Elinor 101, 108
Lévi-Strauss, Claude 60, 64

Lewis, Jayne 119
Lindsay, Alexander 31, 47, 99
Locke, John 2, 7, 17, 18, 26–28, 30, 31, 67–69, 83, 91, 93, 94, 100, 103, 107, 116–19, 121

Macheski, Delmar 99
Mackenzie, D. F. 119
Mackenzie, Scott 103, 105, 117
Mainwaring, Arthur 39
Mandeville, Bernard 19, 30, 41
Markley, Robert 99
marriage 1–5, 7, 9–13, 20, 21, 24, 28, 48, 59–61, 79, 84, 91, 92, 96, 98, 101, 107, 109, 110, 112–14, 122
Marvell, Andrew 124
Meriton, L. 48
Menestrier, François 69, 83, 84
Montgomery, James 47, 48
Motteux, Peter 7, 14
Mountfort, William 10, 14
Mullet, Charles Mullet 48, 63

naming 1, 4, 27, 28, 43, 44, 55, 78, 102, 106, 109, 111
Newman, Richard 104, 118
Novak, Maximillian E. 30, 45, 46, 48, 99, 100, 119
Nussbaum, Felicity 98, 100

Ogg, David 5, 13
Owen, Susan 45

Patriarchy 68, 103, 105, 117, 118, 128
Patterson, Annabel 119
Perception 17, 21, 26, 29, 87–94, 98
Peters, Julia Stone 6
Pincus, Steve xii, 6, 117
Pocock, J. G. A. 117
Powell, George 11, 14, 54, 63
Phillips, John 8, 14
Prager, Jeffrey 99
Prynne, William 24, 31, 114, 115
Pufendorf, Samuel 21, 30

Racine, Jean 116
reputation 1, 3, 4, 7, 13, 22, 25, 43, 44, 46, 78, 88, 103, 106, 114, 118, 119

INDEX 131

Richardson, Mr. 48
Ridpath, George 31
Robb, Nisca 64
Roper, Alan 46
Rymer, Thomas 89, 99

Saint-Evremond, Charles de 12, 14
scandal 1, 3, 4, 5, 6, 9, 12, 42, 67–84, 97, 106, 110, 114
Schneider, Ben Ross 64
Schochet, Gordon 117
Somers, John 118
Shadwell, Thomas 10, 11, 14, 40
Shakespeare, William 1, 27, 28, 29, 31, 43, 51, 55, 90, 92, 98, 99
Sherlock, William 43, 44, 48, 49, 53, 56, 63, 87, 88, 99
Southerne, Thomas 7, 8, 12, 17, 34, 39, 45, 47, 57, 58, 98, 109, 118
Spence, Joseph 49
Sprat, Thomas 124
Staves, Susan 13
Steele, Richard 108, 118, 121
Stone, Lawrence 118
Strawson, Galen 30

Taylor, D. Crane 38, 47

Underwood, Dale 57, 64

Van Bleeck, Richard ii, 16, 18, 21, 30, 119
Vanbrugh, John 5, 7, 8, 9, 14, 16, 17, 18, 19, 20, 21, 25, 26, 30, 58, 119
Velissariou, Aspasia 31
Verbruggen, John 101, 102
vision 2, 11, 18, 39, 44, 47, 52, 70, 72, 75, 94–98, 107, 115, 117

Waller, Edmund 124
Walsh, William 12, 14
Warburton, William 83
Ward, Edward 48
Watt, Ian 14
Weber, Harold 52, 63
Wildi, Max 103
William and Mary 5, 25, 26, 30, 34, 35, 37, 43, 46, 53, 56, 58, 61, 88, 96, 103
Williams, Aubrey 2, 52, 54, 57, 58, 60, 63, 64, 87, 99
Winn, James Anderson 36, 40, 46
Wright, James 6
Wright, Thomas 14, 24
Wycherley, William 5, 41, 57, 60, 64

Zimbardo, Rose 57, 64

www.ingramcontent.com/pod-product-compliance
Lightning Source LLC
Chambersburg PA
CBHW021833300426
44114CB00009BA/422